Slaveiko Gospodinov

Fundamentals of applied geoinformatics

Slaveiko Gospodinov

Fundamentals of applied geoinformatics

ScienciaScripts

Cover image: www.ingimage.com

This book is a translation from the original published under ISBN 978-620-7-46048-9.

Publisher:
Sciencia Scripts
is a trademark of
Dodo Books Indian Ocean Ltd. and OmniScriptum S.R.L publishing group

120 High Road, East Finchley, London, N2 9ED, United Kingdom
Str. Armeneasca 28/1, office 1, Chisinau MD-2012, Republic of Moldova, Europe
Printed at: see last page
ISBN: 978-620-8-28265-3

Contents

Introduction

Geoinformatics is aimed at the development and application of methods for the study of spatial objects and phenomena. Geoinformatics is closely related to a number of sciences and develops on the basis of interaction with these sciences. Geoinformatics studies spatial and temporal processes, phenomena and systems on the Earth's surface and in near-Earth space. Geoinformatics is aimed at the development and application of methods for the study of spatial objects and phenomena. Geoinformatics is closely related to a number of sciences and develops on the basis of interaction with these sciences. Directions of geoinformatics development are shown in Fig.1

Fig.1. Directions of geoinformatics development

The main parts of geoinformatics are "general geoinformatics" [1], "applied geoinformatics" [2, 3] and geoinformatics as an industry [4]. General geoinformatics is developed in two directions: geoinformatics as the science of space [5, 6] and geoinformatics as the integration of earth sciences [7-9]. General geoinformatics is a section of geoinformatics dealing with the research and development of scientific foundations, concept, generalised analysis of geoinformatics and geographic information systems. Applied geoinformatics solves applied problems and studies applied systems, including geotechnical systems/

Modern applied geoinformatics and applied computer science [10] are important for solving applied problems. Geoinformatics is related to cognitive science, mathematical modelling; mathematical logic, linguistics, semiotics, information theory, situational control theory, artificial intelligence systems with metamodelling, and systems theory. Modern geoinformatics uses models of information space and information field.

There are many definitions of geoinformatics. One of the fundamental definitions is given in the encyclopaedia [4]. Geoinformatics [4] is understood as a scientific and technical complex that combines the same name branch of scientific knowledge, technology and applied activities that are associated with the collection, storage, processing and display of spatial data, as well as with the design, creation and operation of GIS. Quite a lot of works are devoted to the problems of geoinformatics [11-24].

We can talk about two groups of main tasks solved by geoinformatics: development of models that form a picture of the world; design, development and maintenance of systems, models, projects in other scientific areas. The main information system in geoinformatics is a geographic information system (GIS). However, it does not exclude the use of other systems.

Modern geoinformatics is characterised by the application of artificial intelligence methods [25] and intelligent GIS [26]. The trend of emergence and development of "smart cities" also affects property management technologies and management theory. Smart cities use artificial intelligence methods, geoinformatics and management theory. Intelligent transport systems are widely used in transport management [27], which are also related to applied geoinformatics. Modern applied geoinformatics has geoinformation resources [28] that can be used in management

Harmonious and sustainable development of modern society is inseparable from the effective use of information and geoinformation resources to meet the needs of the population. Resource optimisation is important and complex from the point of view of sustainable development.

CHAPTER 1

1. Geoinformatics in the system of sciences

1.1. Informatics and geoinformatics

Geoinformatics and informatics [29] can be compared with each other and with other sciences to emphasise the differences and similarities between them. It is useful to compare the information approach and the geoinformation approach as different tools for exploring the world around us.

Computer science originated as the science of programming (computer science) and the science of information processing [30]. The term "informatics" originated in the 1960s in France to name the field of automated information processing as a merger of the French words information and automatique [31].

Informatics is interpreted [31] as the science of how to obtain, accumulate, store, transform, transmit, protect and use information. At the same time, the term "information" was not associated with any subject area, but is a generalisation of information as an *object of* computer *processing*. For quite a long time this term was used as an alternative to the term programming.

The object of informatics research is information processing methods, computer models, algorithms for analysis and computation - without regard to the field of use of this information. It should be emphasised that computer science is concerned with information processing, not information theory. From this point of view, computer science is an intermediary between mathematics and logic on the one hand and applied sciences on the other. It emerged and develops as a science of information processing without having *its own* application. Figure 1.1 shows the relationship between computer science and other sciences. The application of informatics in any field is based on the *specialisation* of informatics to the methods, tasks and data of that subject area. As a result of such specialisation, specific informatics in this subject area appears (Fig. 1.1).

Specialisation of informatics arises on the basis of *adaptation of* informatics in relation to the subject area. In this case, the vector of specialised informatics changes. The main thing for it is not information processing (dominant of informatics), but solving problems of the subject area using informatics.

Fig.1.1 Informatics and its interrelation with other sciences

Any specialised informatics is first of all the solution of special problems of the subject area (e.g. medicine or biology) and secondly only information processing. In informatics, data is processed. The application of data in informatics is shown in Fig.1.2. Data of the subject area are transformed into models of the subject area. As a result, they have specificity reflecting the features of this subject area.

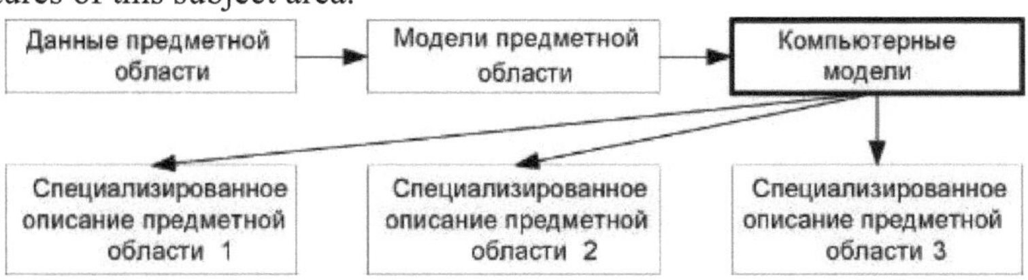

Fig.1.2 Data in computer science as a tool for describing different subject areas

To process models of the subject area, they are transformed into computer models, which are used in computer science. For informatics all data are equivalent, they represent a set of the form *D(A1, A2, A3,.... An)*. Here *D* - data, *A* - qualitatively homogeneous groups of data. As a result of processing, *specialised sets of ban* as a description of objects, phenomena, processes for each subject area are obtained. The paradigm of informatics application is reflected by the chain of

Subject matter data Subject matter models ^■ Computer models Specialised datasets

Unlike informatics, geoinformatics emerged on the basis of two directions: integration of Earth sciences (geo); methods of information processing (Fig.

1.3). The objective need for integration of Earth sciences: geodesy, photogrammetry, cartography, remote sensing of the Earth - existed long ago, independently of informatics.

Informatics was the connecting computational link of integration of sciences into geoinformatics. The basis of technological integration of geoinformatics was CAD technologies as a system of layer-by-layer graphical processing of information in Earth sciences. Thus, it became possible to integrate Earth sciences into a unified system of sciences. This *integrated system of* Earth *sciences* is called geoinformatics.

Let us note the first important difference between the application of informatics and the application of geoinformatics. In subject areas informatics is applied as a tool of specialisation. Geoinformatics is applied as a tool of integration. Informatics specialises processing, while geoinformatics integrates technologies and methods of processing a variety of information into a single technological system.

Along with geoinformatics there is informatics in geodesy, informatics in geology, informatics in photogrammetry, informatics in cartography. But unlike geoinformatics, these are specialised sciences that were created on the basis of differentiation of processing methods, while geoinformatics was created on the basis of integration of data, methods and technologies [7, 8, 32].

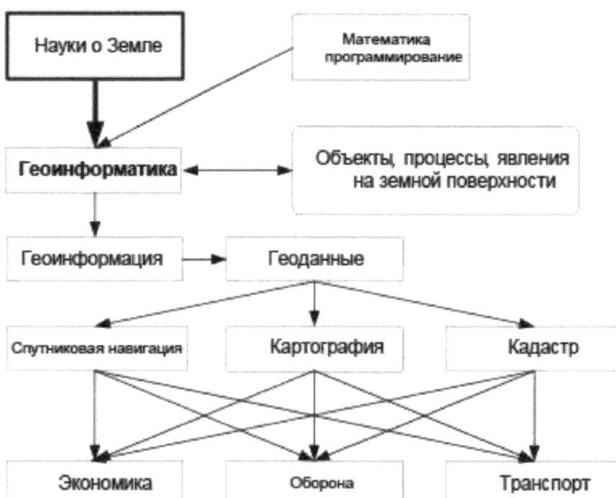

Fig.1.3 Geoinformatics and its relationship with other sciences

It is interesting to compare the application of topology in geoinformatics and computer science. In computer science, topology is applied in the algorithmic aspect as a tool for analysing information flows. In geoinformatics, topology is applied in the algorithmic aspect as a tool for processing geoinformation and in the spatial aspect as a tool for spatial analysis.

Data in informatics is collected by the tools of the subject area in which it is applied. In informatics, data are specialised data, intended to solve specialised problems only in this subject area. For example, informatics in geodesy is designed to solve problems in the field of geodesy using information systems and information technology and does not solve problems in the field of cartography, photogrammetry, space surveying, cadastre, land monitoring, etc.

Geodata collection in geoinformatics is carried out by a wide range of different technologies: aerial and ground photogrammetry, geodesy, GNSS, space methods, cartography, geostatistics, statistics and so on. In geoinformatics, there is a large variety of primary data that are preprocessed. Pre-processing is carried out in the field of geoinformatics. It includes unification of various data, correction by methods of geoinformatics and integration of data into a single environment, introduction of topology and associative links.

Geoinformatics data used in processing are integrated data intended for use in different fields. For example, integrated data in GIS allows solving problems in the field of cartography, photogrammetry, space imagery, in the field of cadastre, ecology, etc.

1.2. Geodesy, geoinformatics and geometry

Geoinformatics is related to geodesy and geometry. Geodesy makes it possible to collect information in geoinformatics using geodetic methods. Geometry makes it possible to carry out spatial modelling in geoinformatics to form spatial knowledge.

To begin with, it is necessary to give an analysis of the relationship between geodesy and geometry. A well-known fact is the transformation of "geometry" and "geodesy". The term "geometry" (geo - Earth, metrio - measurement) means the measurement of the Earth, "geodesy" means the division of the Earth [4]. This interpretation oriented geodesy to the solution of cadastre tasks. Initially it was assumed that geometry would solve measurement problems on the Earth's surface, i.e. those that geodesy currently solves. For this reason, an international federation called Federation Internationale des Geometres (FIG) was established in Paris in 1878. This translates as the international federation of geometers.

At present, foreign universities continue to graduate specialists with the qualification "geometer". Compared to Russian specialists, these geometers perform the functions of surveyors and have no significant relation to the development of mathematics and geometry.

In the course of time, a transformation took place - geometry became a section of mathematics and a theoretical science. Geodesy became a practical science related to the measurement and study of the Earth's surface and the study of spatial techniques of real space. That is why nowadays in foreign and Russian sources FIG is called as International Federation of Surveyors. Abbreviations coincide, but the essence is different. However, the connection between geometry and geodesy exists and it should be taken into account when analysing the concept of geodesy and the tasks of geodesy as a science.

The Development of Geodesy. In-depth studies of the development of geodesy are given in Vanicek's book "Geodesy: Concepts" [33]. The author states that the first geodesic works were carried out in the times of Sumerians, in Ancient China, in Ancient Egypt, in Ancient Greece and in the Roman Empire. It should be noted that the domestic literature mentions geodetic works of Ancient Egypt and Ancient Rome, but does not talk about geodetic works in Ancient China, where they were carried out earlier and used specific methods and special measuring tools. The development of navigation revealed the need to determine the shape of the Earth. This task was solved by the methods of astronomy and geodesy. In the process of making geodetic instruments, the connection between geodesy and other sciences appeared: physics, optics, mathematics. It should be noted that abroad geodesy is considered as a section of applied mathematics. In Russia, these sciences are separated.

Geometry. As a branch of science, geometry is currently a branch of mathematics that studies spatial structures and spatial relations [34-37]. Geometry studies the mutual arrangement of bodies, which also studies spatial knowledge [38-41].

Euclidean geometry studies figures in the plane and in space, and calculates their areas and volumes. Geoinformatics does the same, based on geometric methods. The coordinate method proposed by Descartes in 1637 formed the basis of analytical and differential geometry, and the problems associated with drawing led to the creation of descriptive and projective geometry. In geoinformatics and geodesy, the coordinate method serves as the basis for the creation of coordinate support [42-44].

Differential geometry and differential topology are two related branches of mathematics that study smooth manifolds. They have many applications in geoinformatics. In differential topology, structures are considered that have identical neighbourhoods for any pair of points. In differential geometry, there may be local invariants (curvature) that vary at points. Curvature is explored in spatial models in geoinformatics.

It is worth mentioning the language of spatial aggregation [45], which develops the ideas of geometry in the field of abstract spatial relations. It describes the mutual arrangement of bodies, which is expressed by touching or adjoining each other, by the arrangement "between", "inside". The theory of geometry is based on abstractions and abstract forms. A distinction is made between point, moulded, area and volume bodies. This division is used in geoinformatics. it serves as a basis for the classification of geoinformation models. We can talk about the development of geometry ideas in geoinformatics.

There is no earth (geo) and no earth measurements in modern geometry. It is a mathematical science, despite the "geo" part. The content of any science, including geometry and geodesy, is determined not on the basis of its original name, but on the basis of the problems it solves. For geometry, these are mathematical problems. For geodesy, the situation is similar. Many interpretations of geodesy have long excluded its second part "division". Satellite and space geodesy have emerged.

Common in geoinformatics, geometry and geodesy are: study of space, study of spatial relations, study of spatial forms, study of mutual arrangement of bodies.

There are differences. Geometry studies abstract spaces, geodesy studies real space, geoinformatics studies abstract and real spaces. Geodesic measurements contain errors. Information in geoinformatics contains errors

Geodesy includes Euclidean geometry as a mathematical foundation. Geoinformatics includes Euclidean geometry as a mathematical foundation and also includes differential geometry and differential topology. Error handling is a branch of probability theory that is part of the subject matter of geodesy and geoinformatics.

The development of geodesy allows us to state the following. Geodesy methods are applicable on the Earth's natural satellite - the Moon, on Mars on a small celestial body. The area of application of geodesy is much wider than the surface of the Earth. It is applicable on all solid celestial bodies and the Earth is one of such bodies. There is space geodesy [46-48], geodetic astronomy [49-52], satellite geodesy [53]. There is space geoinformatics [54, 55].

Consequently, there is no reason to associate geodesy and geoinformatics only with the Earth. The field of application of geodesy [56] and geoinformatics is real space. Geodesy and geoinformatics are the sciences of space. They can explore terrestrial space, near-Earth space, underground space, space of any planet.

1.3. Geotechnical systems as an object of geoinformatics research

The peculiarity of many scientific and applied directions is the use of the concept of "geotechnical system" (GTS) meaningfully and linguistically [57-

59]. Taking into account modern concepts of systems and complex systems, a number of interpretations of the concept of geotechnical system do not meet modern concepts and are contradictory. It is especially important for geoinformatics and in geoinformatics of transport. The concept of geotechnical system is associated with the concept of geotechnical object and geotechnical monitoring, the scope of which is wider than the concept of geotechnical system. Therefore, it is advisable to analyse the modern representation of geotechnical system and introduce the concept of geotechnical system, which does not contradict the already introduced, but complements them.

The first definitions of the concept of geotechnical system (GTS) were introduced by specialists in geography and ecology in isolation from the concepts of system analysis and complex system. For example, the BSE [60] provides a definition with a geographical context. Let us highlight the key points.

1. "GEOTECHNICAL SYSTEM, a special geographical class of natural-technical systems".
2. It is further stated that natural and engineering objects in HS are interconnected and function as a whole.
3. The GTS is an open system.
4. The following heterogeneous list [61] is included as examples of HTS: landscapes, meteorological instruments, hydrological instruments, manned spacecraft, and others.
5. Information on the state of GTS subsystems is an integral part of geo-ecological monitoring.
6. "Natural processes in landscapes are often determined by the functioning of the geotechnical system."

It follows from paragraph 4 that the spacecraft and the meteorological instrument fall into the same typological range

It follows from paragraph 1 and 4 that the spacecraft and the meteorological instrument belong to a geographical class

Punta 5 relates GTS only to geo-environmental monitoring. This is a very narrow approach, as apart from environmental monitoring there are other types of monitoring investigating geotechnical systems: geomonitoring geo-information monitoring, space monitoring, geotechnical monitoring and others.

Tying a spaceship to a geographic class is pretty bold. The moon has more reason to be tied to Earth than a spaceship. A spaceship is assembled on Earth. It then leaves the Earth's surface and enters near-Earth space. From near-Earth space, it can travel to sublunar and beyond moon space. A spaceship can travel to Mars or other planets and even go beyond the solar system. Therefore, it is incorrect to relate it to the class of geographical systems. However, regardless of its location, a spacecraft can be considered a geotechnical system. It is of terrestrial origin and created by human hands.

Many definitions consider HS as a special "geographical class" of natural-technical systems. This does not apply to all systems. For example, a landscape can be natural (natural) and artificial (with anthropogenic elements). Both landscapes are geographical systems. However, the appearance of the term anthropogenic instead of technical is important in this reasoning. There are landscapes that are not geotechnical systems. For example, the landscape of Mars is not a geographic system. It is a Martian natural system.

The term geotechnical system does not necessarily have to be associated only with technical systems. There is a concept of object designation and a concept of object meaning. The designation does not always coincide exactly with the meaning. Many terms are not understood literally, but with a certain meaning. For example, fuzzy sets are not fuzzy but are probabilistic. The term "regression line" in mathematics denotes not only the process of regression, but also the process of progression or the absence of both.

Therefore, the term "geotechnical system" should be interpreted on the basis of its modern semantic content and designation of those objects or systems to which this term is applied. Let us consider the relationship between the concepts of system and aggregate.

The Geography Dictionary defines a geotechnical system as "*a set of* natural objects and technical structures", "in close co-operation". This definition does not contain systemic features or attributes of a system.

Geotechnical systems [61-66] are an objective reality of the surrounding world. There is geotechnical engineering [67, 68], geotechnical modelling [69], geotechnical models [70]. Despite the large number of studies, geotechnical systems have not yet been systematised as well. Geotechnical systems have been researched more in geotechnical engineering, geology, ecology [71], natural resource extraction [72] and environmental protection. Geotechnical systems serve as the basis for obtaining both spatial knowledge and geo-knowledge [73, 74]. However, with the advent of geoinformatics and the development of complex systems theory, geotechnical systems have been viewed from a different perspective. Geotechnical systems are investigated in the field of artificial intelligence [75].

Two directions of development of geotechnical systems. In geology and ecology the concept of geotechnical system (GTS) was treated as a natural-technical system (NTS) [76-78]. A geotechnical system in this field is a set of engineering structures and the associated part of the geological environment in the zone of influence that has clear boundaries. In this aspect, the geological or ecological environment is considered in interaction with engineering structures as a part of the overall system. the paradigm of this approach is as follows

Part of the environment + engineering structures natural technical system. (1)

The main thing in this paradigm of connection and interaction of parts among and structures [79]. The issue of GTS integrity has been sidelined. The main thing in this paradigm is geotechnics. Geotechnics investigates soil formation, classification and investigation of soil variability, strength and deformation of engineering structures, water flow through the soil mass, soil settlement and compaction, retaining structures, slope stability, foundations and soil treatment for engineering purposes. Geotechnical systems of this type can be referred to as GTS1.

From the position of system analysis [80], if GTS is a system, it is a type of complex systems. In this case, it falls into the typological range of complex systems along with data systems [81], organisational systems [82], technological systems [83, 84], technical systems [85], complex organisational and technical systems [86], and cybernetic systems. The paradigm of this approach is as follows

Artificial systems + external environment geotechnical system (2)

The main thing in this paradigm is the connections [87] and integrity of the system. The main thing in this paradigm is the relationships and integrity of the system and the interactions between a part of the environment and its environment in the aspect of the dynamics of GTS development and its influence on the whole environment. The second paradigm is more related to geoinformatics. than to geology or geodynamics. This opens up a number of opportunities for GTS. Geoinformatics technologies are used in decision support [88]. GIS is being used to study GTS [89]. This creates management opportunities for GTS built on GIS. Geotechnical systems of this type can be called GTS2

Comparing GTS to a complex system requires the introduction of a complexity indicator. Such an indicator is the geotechnical category. It is defined as a category of complexity of an engineering object in the aspect of foundation and foundation design. An important factor is geotechnical monitoring [91, 90], which is considered as a kind of geomonitoring [92. 93]

The built environment serves as a dynamic interface through which human society and the ecosystem interact and influence each other. Understanding this interdependence is key to understanding sustainability as it applies to civil engineering. There is a growing consensus that ensuring a sustainable built environment begins with incorporating sustainability ideas into the planning and design phases of an infrastructure construction project. Geotechnical engineering can significantly impact the sustainability of infrastructure development because of its early position in the construction process. Geotechnical engineering provides the foundation for sustainable civil infrastructure development. Examples of GTS1 are tailings dams, quarries, mineral deposits mines. Their main objective is to interact correctly with nature Examples of GTS2 are railway bridges, dams, subways, railway tracks. Their main purpose is to solve a technical or technological problem while minimising the impact on nature.

Applications of computer science and geoinformatics in GTS. GTS is investigated in applied computer science and applied geoinformatics. GTS can be considered as an applied system [94]. The basis for collecting information about GTS is geomonitoring, which relies on geoinformatics monitoring [95]. The semiotic approach [96, 97] and the information units method [98] are used to build spatial models for GTS. The basis of processing in geomonitoring is geodata [99, 100]. Fact-fixing models are formed on the basis of primary data. Thematic geodata contain geotechnical characteristics. Geodata allow generalisation, which enables metamodelling [101].

The advent of the big data era [102-107] has brought additional challenges to GTS. It has led to research in the field of artificial intelligence (AI). AI algorithms are characterised by powerful feature and expression learning capabilities compared to traditional machine learning (ML) methods, which has attracted researchers from all over the world from different fields to its increasing application. In addition, in the field of geological engineering, AI has been widely applied in various research areas. Four major algorithms including feedforward neural (FNN), recurrent neural network (RNN), convolutional neural network (CNN) and generative adversarial network (GAN) along with their geotechnical applications have been elaborated [107] Geotechnical engineering deals with soils, rocks and their use in engineering structures. By their nature, soils and rocks exhibit complex behaviour and high levels of uncertainty in material modelling. Artificial Intelligence (AI) methods have been developed and utilised by an increasing number of researchers in geotechnical engineering over the last three decades. These methods are considered successful due to their ability to predict complex nonlinear relationships. The paper [108], based on more than one thousand literature sources, presented a detailed review of the effectiveness of artificial intelligence methods and algorithms used in geotechnical engineering. Nine key areas where the application of AI techniques is most prominent were identified: frozen soils and thermal properties of soils, rock mechanics, earthworks and pavements, landslides and ground liquefaction, slope stability, shallow and pile foundations, tunnelling machines, dams and unsaturated soils. Artificial neural networks have become a widely used AI technique.

Life Cycle Assessment (LCA) is important for GTS, but has so far had limited application in the geotechnical engineering discipline. That said, the life cycle model I it is widely applied to real estate and civil engineering projects such as pavements and roads. Life cycle assessment for GTS requires the development or refinement of environmental indicators, impact categories and causal pathways. Environmental indicators they relate to geotechnical factors, especially those related to soil quality, soil functions and the ecosystem services provided by soils. Many existing geotechnical methods arise from land use and land use change studies related to other disciplines (e.g. agriculture). For applicability to geotechnical projects, the resolution of many of these methods and the resulting indicators must be reduced from the landscape/macro scale to the project scale. In the near future, geotechnical LCA practitioners should begin to track changes in soil properties and qualitatively report impacts on land and soil resources. and causal relationships are needed as they relate to geotechnical applications, especially those related to soil quality, soil functions, and ecosystem services. Geotechnical systems [109-113] continue to evolve, but their final theory is far from complete

1.4 Geoinformatics and geomatics

In some countries geomatics [114] has been understood as a synonym for geoinformatics, in others it is used as a derivation of geoinformatics [115-117]. The reasons for this are partly different national linguistic peculiarities and the difference in the level of Earth sciences development. The higher the level of Earth sciences, the higher the importance of geoinformatics. The technical committee of the international standardisation organisation ISO/TC 211 on geodata and geoinformation uses these as synonyms [118]. However, it is noted that there are some differences in the development of these scientific areas. The International Conference on Education in Geodesy, Cadastre and Land Management: Trends of Globalisation and Convergence held at MIIGAiK in September 2012 put everything in its place [119, 120]. It turned out that geomatics is an application of geoinformatics in the field of land user. Abroad, geomatics is defined as the art and science of land surveying. A geomatics specialist is a cadastral engineer with good training in the field of spatial information processing with the help of information systems and

technologies.
Geoinformatics is terminologically closely related to earth sciences and secondarily to computer science. In terms of applications, geoinformatics is widely used in other fields. Therefore, it is reasonable to consider its development from different aspects. Modern geoinformatics is more space science than Earth science
There are two trends in the development of geoinformatics. The first trend is integration, which makes geoinformatics an interdisciplinary science. The second trend is differentiation. There is general geoinformatics, applied geoinformatics and special geoinformatics. Transport geoinformatics and space geoinformatics have emerged and are developing. This extended development requires periodic analyses and updates of the main provisions of geoinformatics.
Geoinformatics links social and economic information processing methods with various fields of science and practical applications. Geoinformatics is used in medicine, artificial intelligence, management, education, agriculture and ecology. Geoinformatics serves as a basis for geomonitoring.
One of the features of geoinformatics is the use of models for processing. In this case, models are divided into two categories: models for processing in GIS [121] and applied models for solving applied problems
[122].
Another feature of geoinformatics is the use of a special kind of data - geodata. This data is structured and creates great opportunities for its use and model building.
The third feature of geoinformatics is that spatial relations are among the objects of its study along with physical objects and processes. Spatial relations exist in real space on the Earth's surface, in near-Earth space and in outer space. This once again defines geoinformatics as a science of space.
The fourth feature of geoinformatics is the recent application of information situation models [123-125] and situational modelling on this basis [126]. One of the directions of geoinformatics research is geoinformation systems and technologies and their applications.
The fifth feature of geoinformatics is the presence in it of a special type of modelling - geoinformation modelling
The sixth feature of geoinformatics is the presence in it of a special type of monitoring geoinformation monitoring and geomonitoring. Geoinformatics can be considered as a system of sciences and continues to develop successfully as a system.
Geomatics is defined in the ISO/TC 211 series of standards as "the discipline

concerned with the collection, dissemination, storage, analysis, processing, presentation of geographic data or geographic information" [127]. [127]. According to another definition, it "consists of products, services and tools related to the collection, integration and management of geographic (geospatial) data". It is also known as geomatics engineering (geomatics engineering) geodesy and geoinformatics engineering (geodesy and geoinformatics engineering) or geospatial engineering (geospatial engineering). Geodesy engineering was the commonly used name for geomatics engineering in the past

There is a long-known conflict between French-speaking scientists and English-speaking scientists. Geomatics is partly a product of this conflict. French-speaking scientists are constantly trying to invent terms as an alternative to English terms, even if it is not useful or contrary to common sense.

The term "geomatique" was coined in French ("geomatique") in the late 1960s by the scientist Bernard Dubuisson to reflect (in his view) recent developments in the work of the surveyor and photogrammetrist [128]. The basic idea was to exclude informatics and reduce its importance in science that is related to the earth sciences. Geoinformatics is an unfortunate name that is literally interpreted often incorrectly. Geoinformatics is an integrated earth science in which informatics is used occasionally and has no more than 10% importance there. The importance of geodesy in geoinformatics is an order of magnitude higher than that of informatics.

The term "geomatics" was first used in a memorandum from the French Ministry of Public Works dated 1 June 1971 establishing a "permanent committee on geomatics" in the government [129].

The introduction of a term to diminish the meaning of informatics should be considered reasonable. Its introduction in French is a subjective whim of French-speaking scholars. It is therefore logical that the term was popularised in English. This was done by the French-Canadian geodesist Michel Paradis in his article The Little Geodesist, which took place in 1981 and in a keynote address at the congress celebrating the centenary of the Canadian Geodetic Institute (now known as the Canadian Institute of Geomatics) in 1981. April 1982 Paradis argued that at the end of the 20th century the needs for geographic information would reach unprecedented levels in history and that to meet these needs it was necessary to combine both traditional disciplines of land surveying and new tools and techniques for data collection, processing, storage and dissemination into a new discipline [130]. This is relevant to geoinformatics and geomatics.

The link between both sciences is geographic information and spatial information [131]. Geographers also messed up in the development of geoinformatics and geomatics, but geographic information is still more important than informatics.
Geographic Information Systems are often erroneously referred to as Geographic Information Systems. There is no geography in GIS. The main information in GIS is geodetic information. Even geographic coordinate systems are not used in GIS. Topographers, geodesists, cartographers, photogrammetrists, transport specialists, cadastre specialists, managers work with GIS, but not geographers.
Geomatics (like geoinformatics, there is no difference) includes the tools and techniques used in topographic surveying, remote sensing, cartography, geographic information systems (GIS), global navigation satellite systems (GPS, GLONASS, Galileo, Compass), photogrammetry, geophysics, geography and related forms of Earth mapping. This term was originally used in Canada, but was later adopted by the International Organization for Standardization, Royal Institution of Chartered Surveyors (hence the divergence in application), Many other international (English-speaking) organisations (especially in the United States) have preferred the term geospatial technology [132]. They treat this term as synonymous with the composite term "geospatial information and communication technology" [1133].
Formally, the fields of geoinformatics and geomatics are common, but over time and in its practical application, the term has been almost exclusively restricted to surveying.
Geoinformatics has been proposed as an alternative comprehensive term, but its use is common only in some parts of the world, especially in Europe. Formally, there is no difference between the terms geoinformatics and geomatics. There is a difference in the language of the term and in the field of application. Geomatics is mainly used for the surface of the earth. And geoinformatics has turned into the science of space.
Along with geoinformatics and geomatics, the term "spatial sciences" is proposed. The term "spatial science" or spatial sciences is mainly used in Australia. Australian universities that offer spatial science degrees include Curtin University [134], University of Tasmania [135], University of Adelaide [136], University of Melbourne [137] and RMIT University [138]
Spatial information professionals in the Asia-Pacific region are represented by a professional body called the Surveying and Spatial Science Institute (SSSI). Geomatic engineering, or geospatial engineering, is a rapidly growing

engineering discipline that focuses on spatial information (i.e., location-based information). Location is the primary factor used to integrate a very wide range of data for spatial analysis and visualisation. Geomatics engineers apply engineering principles to spatial information and implement relational data structures using measurement sciences, thus utilising geomatics and acting as spatial information engineers. Geomatics engineers manage local, regional, national, and global spatial data infrastructures. Geomatic engineering also includes aspects of computer engineering, software engineering and civil engineering

Thus, a geomatics engineer can be involved in an extremely wide range of information gathering activities and applications. Geomatic engineers design, develop and operate systems to collect and analyse spatial information about the earth, oceans, natural resources and man-made objects.

The more traditional geodetic part of geomatics engineering is concerned with defining and recording the boundaries and areas of real estate parcels, as well as preparing and interpreting legal descriptions of land. Tasks more closely related to civil engineering include the design and layout of public infrastructure and urban subdivisions, as well as mapping and control surveys for construction projects.

Geomatics engineers serve society by collecting, tracking, archiving, and maintaining a variety of spatial data infrastructures. Geomatic engineers use a wide range of technologically advanced tools such as digital total stations with theodolites / range finders, global positioning system (GPS) equipment, digital aerial photographs (both satellite and aerial), and computer-based geographic information systems (GIS). These tools enable the geomatic engineer to collect, process, analyse, analyse, visualise and manage spatially related information to solve a wide range of technical and social problems.

Geomatic Engineering is a field of activity that combines the collection, processing, analysis, display and management of spatial information. It is an exciting and new subject group in spatial and environmental information sciences with a wide range of employment opportunities, as well as offering challenging pure and applied research tasks in a wide range of interdisciplinary areas.

In different schools and in different countries, the same curriculum is taught under the name geodesy in some schools and under the names geomatics, engineering geodesy, geomatics engineering, geospatial (information) engineering, geodesy engineering or geodesy and geoinformatics in others. While these professions were once often taught in civil engineering curricula, more and more universities are including departments related to geodata science in utj informatics, computer science or applied mathematics. These facts demonstrate the breadth, depth and scope of the highly interdisciplinary nature of geomatics engineering. The geoscientific engineering job is well established in the US military [139, 140].

Geomatics and geoinformatics at first had the same field of study aimed at solving problems on the Earth's surface. Both sciences investigate technologies for acquiring and processing spatial data. Over time, the emphasis of geomatics has been related to the scientific basis of land use. Geomatics is dominated by the engineering aspect. Geoinformatics is dominated by the aspect of space exploration including outer space. The research direction of geomatics refers mainly to the fields of measurement processing and spatial information processing technologies for solving land use problems. In terms of application, *geomatics* has a more applied orientation, while *geoinformatics* includes fundamental and theoretical foundations. Common to both sciences is the construction of research based on the integration of knowledge from other disciplines and the development of theoretical foundations for themselves based on relevant basic sciences.

Geomatics is a field that encompasses several others, such as the older field of engineering land surveying, as well as many other aspects of spatial data management, ranging from data science and cartography to geography. Following advanced developments in digital data processing, the nature of the tasks required of the professional land surveyor has changed considerably in recent years, and for an increasing number of people the term 'surveying' no longer accurately encompasses the full range of tasks that the profession performs. deals with. As our societies become more complex, information with its associated spatial location is becoming increasingly important for decision making from both personal, business, community and large-scale government perspectives.

In addition to geoinformatics and geomatics, other names such as spatial science or geospatial science are used. However, terminological differences do not always correspond to substantive differences.

CHAPTER 2

2. Development and application of applied geoinformatics

The direction of geoinformatics related to the development of technology and systems for studying and managing processes and phenomena of the surrounding world as an applied direction led to the creation of a special direction - applied geoinformatics. Applied geoinformatics has two directions of development. Independent development and application for solving applied problems on the basis of integration of mathematics, informatics and Earth sciences. The second direction is related to the support and development of specialised geoinformatics.

Within the framework of the second direction, a new direction in economics - spatial economics - appeared [141-143]. Within the framework of the second direction the following sciences appeared: logistic geoinformatics [144], ecological geoinformatics [145-147], economic geoinformatics [148], transport geoinformatics [149-152], space geoinformatics [153]. Environmental geoinformatics is also called geoecology [154].

2.1. Space geoinformatics

Space research is aimed at studying the external environment in the form of near and far space. Their peculiarity is that they are based on methods and knowledge obtained in terrestrial conditions and during the exploration of the planet Earth. Earth sciences make a significant contribution to the development of space research. The main basic object of comparison in space research is the Earth. As a planet, it is better studied and all possible measurements can be made on it. The use of Earth research data as an analogue for comparison with other bodies is most common in such sciences as planetary geology, geomorphology and atmospheric sciences. This feature provides a basis for transferring Earth science methods (geoinformatics, geodesy, geodynamics, photogrammetry, cartography) for application in space research. Space research is an important tool for exploring the world around us. Space research is an important component in building a picture of the world. Geoinformatics is also a tool for exploring the world around us and building a picture of the world. This brings geoinformatics and space research closer together. Space research sets the task of acquiring new knowledge and revealing tacit knowledge. Geoinformatics also explores tacit knowledge. Geoinformatics has as one of its main objectives the task of acquiring new knowledge, spatial knowledge and geo-knowledge. This also brings geoinformatics and space research closer together. Modern space research and construction of the world picture are connected with the application of "terrestrial" sciences of geoinformatics, geography, geodesy. Space geodesy, geography of extraterrestrial territories, space geology, geodesic astronomy exist and are applied. The term "small celestial bodies" is used to refer to small planets and asteroids [155], although they are cosmic, not celestial. Geoinformatics as a science that integrates the Earth sciences also has every reason for the term cosmic [52-54, 153]. There are a number of works in geodesy that prove that geodesy is a science of space. This gives reason to believe that geoinformatics can also be considered as a science of space. The specialisation of geoinformatics in space exploration can be space geoinformatics. This term has not yet found wide application. Therefore, in a general sense we can talk about geoinformatics as a tool for space exploration. In a narrow sense we can talk about space geoinformatics. Space geoinformatics (SG) or geoinformatics of space exploration requires the introduction of new methods of analysis due to new tasks and requirements. Space geoinformatics requires research and development of new analytical, algorithmic and technological methods. Unlike space geodesy, space geography, geodetic astronomy, the peculiarity of space geoinformatics is a complex approach to space exploration. This integrated approach is borrowed from terrestrial geoinformatics. Space geoinformatics provides comparability and analysis at the model level. At the technology level, space geoinformatics provides a tool for sharing analysis and processing methods. At the cognitive level, Space Geoinformatics is similar to terrestrial geoinformatics, which promotes the integration of sciences. This property of geoinformatics is transferred to space geoinformatics and makes space geoinformatics a tool for the universal exploration of outer space.

2.2. Logistics geoinformatics

Geoinformatics is applied wherever spatial information is required. The accumulated experience gives grounds to introduce the concept of "logistics geoinformatics" as a field of geoinformatics related to transport and logistics.
From integrative positions geoinformatics can be considered as a system of sciences [156]. From spatial positions geoinformatics can be considered as a science of space. From the consumer position, geoinformatics can be considered as a technology that meets the needs of specialists in different application areas.

There are many definitions [157-159] for logistics, which differ in details but reflect the general essence. The fact that logistics mostly deals with spatial objects and spatial flows is poorly reflected. The spatial factor brings geoinformatics and logistics closer together. Logistics requires management and is a management tool. geoinformatics is used for management. There are logistics systems, many of which can be realised with GIS tools.

From a consumer perspective, geoinformatics can be seen as a technology that

meets the needs of specialists from different application areas. This also brings geoinformatics and logistics closer together.
Logistics operates with forward and reverse flows of goods, commodities, resources, services, information according to the needs of customers. Logistics manages supply chains [160, 161] in such a way that the chain corresponds to the logical chain [162] and the optimal chain in the network. There are military and civilian logistics. Civilian logistics deals with the acquisition, movement and storage of raw materials, semi-finished and finished goods. For service organisations providing services such as rubbish collection, mail delivery, housing and utilities and after-sales services, logistics problems also need to be solved. Logistics contains a significant part of an organisation's or country's operating costs.
Distribution centre management [163] is considered as a field of logistics. From a modelling point of view, there are similarities between operations management and logistics. From a modelling point of view, there are similarities between spatial modelling in geoinformatics and spatial flow modelling in logistics.
Currently, there are many specialisations of logistics. Inbound and outbound logistics are divided according to the direction of flows. Inbound logistics [164] aims to procure and organise the inbound movement of materials, parts or work-in-progress inventory from suppliers to manufacturing or assembly plants, warehouses or retail shops. Outbound logistics (Outbound logistics) [165] relates to the storage and movement of the final product and associated information flows from the end of the production line to the end user.
Logistics can be divided into the following types according to their areas of application: procurement logistics, distribution logistics, after-sales logistics, disposal logistics, global logistics, internal affairs logistics, concierge services, asset management logistics, reverse logistics, point-of-sale materials logistics, emergency logistics, production logistics, construction logistics, capital project logistics, digital logistics, information logistics, and humanitarian logistics. Let's look at some of the types of logistics.
Global logistics [166] is the process of managing material flows through the so-called supply chain from the place of production to other parts of the world. This often requires an intermodal transport system, sea, air, rail and road transport
Advance logistics [167] consists of the activities necessary to design or develop a plan for conducting logistics operations
Procurement logistics [168] includes: market research, requirements planning, make-or-buy decisions, supplier management, order placement and order

control. The objectives in procurement logistics can be contradictory: maximising efficiency by concentrating on core competencies, outsourcing while maintaining company autonomy, or minimising procurement costs while maximising security in the supply process

Distribution logistics solves problems of optimal resource allocation, selection of production locations based on optimisation criteria. It uses the theory of fuzzy sets. A typical example is the Launhardt problem [169].

Distribution logistics [170] (goods distribution logistics) is aimed at delivering finished goods to the consumer. It includes order processing, warehousing and transport. Distribution logistics is necessary because the time, place and quantity of production is different from the time, place and quantity of consumption.

The main function of Disposal logistics [171] is to reduce logistics costs and improve the quality of services related to the disposal of waste generated in the course of a company's operations

Reverse logistics [172] focuses on operations that involve the reuse of products and materials. The process of reverse logistics involves the management and sale of surplus as well as products returned to suppliers from customers. Reverse logistics is all operations that involve the reuse of products and materials. It is "the process of planning, implementing and controlling the efficient and cost-effective flow of raw materials, work-in-progress, finished goods and related information from the point of consumption to the point of origin for the purpose of value recovery or proper disposal. More specifically, reverse logistics is the process of moving goods from their typical final destination for the purpose of value recovery or proper disposal. The opposite of reverse logistics is "forward logistics".

Green logistics [173] includes actions to minimise the environmental impact of logistics activities. This includes all forward and reverse flow activities

Asset control logistics [174] deals with the assets needed to showcase, preserve and promote an organisation's products. Some examples are refrigerators, hoovers, monitors, seasonal equipment, poster stands and frames

Construction logistics [175] has been used for thousands of years. As different human civilisations have tried to build the best possible structures for life and defence. Now construction logistics has become a vital part of construction. Over the past few years, construction logistics has become a separate field of knowledge and research within the subject of supply chain management and logistics.

Logistics of information and computer networks includes actions on network balancing, optimisation of network flow routes, reduction of interference and network dissipation. Mobile network logistics includes actions to optimise station placement and optimise network traffic based on customer density. Global network logistics includes actions on server placement, optimisation of global network flows, reduction of network traffic interference.

Most of the types of logistics considered apply spatial information. Spatial information is processed by geoinformatics. Therefore, the application of geoinformatics in logistics or the formation of logistics geoinformatics increases the efficiency of logistics processes.

2.3. Environmental geoinformatics

The application of geoinformatics in ecology is currently identified with the term "geoecology". Geoecology is a broader concept, but it is based on applied geoinformatics or geoinformatics methods

The term "geoecology" is tied to geographer Carl Troll. He originally introduced it as a synonym for the term "landscape ecology" [176] Its first interpretation defined the objectives of geoecology in "the study of spatial complexes in terms of the relationships and interactions between living communities in a given part of the landscape". Geology plays a fundamental role in shaping the biotic world. Geoecology [177-179] is an interdisciplinary science that integrates the earth sciences with the life sciences, focusing on the multiple influences of geoecological processes on historical and contemporary patterns of biogeography, including the causes and consequences of geoedaphy on biota at all temporal and spatial scales. At this point it is worth noting geoecology's integration of the earth sciences. Geoinformatics does the same. This brings the two sciences closer together. In doing so, geoinformatics acts as an integrator. At the same time, geoecology studies the role of biota in a number of processes, including weathering and pedogenesis, thereby altering the chemical and physical composition of the Earth's surface and its patterns of biodiversity. Geobiology (geobotany and geozoology), biogeography and biogeochemistry are important subfields of geoecology. Evolutionary plant ecology also has its roots in geoecology. Recent advances in spatial information [180], geoinformatics, GIS theory [181] and remote sensing [182] have created the conditions for geomonitoring to be applied in geoecology. The application of laser devices such as LiDAR and satellite images gives a new round of development of ecology. Therefore, the application of geoinformatics in geoecology is topical.

Territories are generally important for nature conservation. The habitats they support are dynamic and fragile.

Territories are vulnerable to the impacts of human activities and respond to anthropogenic change at long-term scales. Biodiversity and conservation values are closely linked to the ecology and condition of an area and it is essential that area management systems are based on an understanding of these linkages

It is possible to introduce the concept of spatial environment in addition to the concept of habitat. A spatial environment is a space, objects in space, without reference to the living world. Such environments and habitats are vulnerable and responsive to climate change.

Analysing the variability of natural processes requires large datasets that can be obtained using geoinformatics methods. These datasets are generated from field measurements, remote sensing and digital elevation model (DEM) analyses. This information allows to obtain geomorphological processing units (GPUs), which are called information units in geoinformatics [183]. They are defined with the help of GIS modelling.

At the first stage of geoinformation research, information models and information resources are formed [184, 185]. The results are placed in databases [186, 187]. or spatial databases 188]. When building models, a semiotic approach is used. It consists in the fact that when building models, the semantics of the object is taken into account and standardised information units are chosen to denote terrain objects and their properties. As a result of model formation and modelling, digital maps [189, 1900] and digital models [191, 192] are created

In the second step, geo-information modelling is carried out and the results of the modelling are also put into databases.

In the third step, qualitative and quantitative analyses are carried out.

^ identify latent variables, reveal tacit knowledge and make predictions. The overall result of ecological research is the acquisition of new knowledge about the ecological state of the territory and the surrounding world.

An important factor and mandatory condition is the creation and use of a single coordinate system [193, 194]. A single coordinate system allows comparing the results of observations obtained in different periods of time. A single coordinate system allows comparing different types of geoinformation measurements and geo-environmental surveys.

There are similarities in the tasks of geoecology and geoinformatics. Geoinformatics is a tool of geoecology to accumulate spatial data. The accumulated database allows quantitative assessment of spatial processes, interaction of processes within the territory. The application of this concept allows the calculation of temporal characteristics. This is due to the fact that geodata in geoinformatics contains the characteristic "time", which allows to study temporal processes and temporal dependencies. Geodata allows the estimation of sediment transport rates and therefore leads to a better understanding of the actual development activities of the geomorphological landscape. In order to extrapolate environmental data in time and space, they are analysed in terms of depth and total volume, primarily using geoinformatics techniques. In this way, the validity of measured patterns and processes for the time scale is assessed.

2.4. Geoinformatics of transport

Geoinformatics of transport emerged long before the emergence of applied geoinformatics. Initially, the scientific discipline that dealt with this direction was called geography of transport networks [195]. It was closely related to transport geography [196]. Geography of transport networks emerged in Germany in the middle of the XIX century. Its founder is considered to be the German Johan Kohl. This geographer investigated the transport networks of Europe Russia, USA and Canada. He generalised the types of transport systems in these countries. On the basis of his research and generalisations, the geography of transport networks emerged. The geography of transport networks was the methodological basis of geoinformatics of transport. In comparison, the methodological basis of conventional geoinformatics was cartography.

Transport geoinformatics has developed on the basis of the integration of transport network geography with earth sciences and logistics. Therefore, along with approaches and methods typical for transport network geography, it has included a number of specialised methods.

Geoinformatics of transport covers land, water and air transport. Land types: railway, road and pipeline; water types - sea and river; air types - aviation. It is also divided into passenger and freight transport. The advantage of transport geoinformatics is the ability to create an integrated information model that combines different types of transport, which is important for intermodal transport. Geoinformation models are models of intermodal transport. In a particular case, they are models of individual modes of transport.

Transport geoinformatics is a specialised applied geoinformatics focused on studying and solving transport problems, called. The tasks of transport are diverse. This leads to the diversification of transport geoinformatics (TG) into the following areas:

- theoretical TG, which includes the development of mathematical and statistical methods for analysing transport network models.
- topological TG , which includes the study of functioning of transport flows and topological optimisation of transport flows. The section of track development falls into this direction,

- controlling TG, which includes controlling and monitoring the condition of transport networks;
- geoinformatics of certain types of transport (railway, road, air, sea, river, pipeline, telecommunications);
- Infrastructure geoinformatics;
- regional transport geoinformatics (description of transport of individual regions and countries);
- space geoinformatics of transport. Which includes the application of space technologies for monitoring and management of transport infrastructure, as well as rolling stock management.
- Logistics geoinformatics.

Common for different directions is system analysis [197-199]. Important key parameters of transport geoinformatics, are: topological network, topological system, system, spatial links and relations, spatial modelling, information modelling, digital models, volumetric models [200]. Transport is a generalised concept. In TG, it is necessary to talk about the transport system, which should be modelled as a complex system. This ensures that the parts of the transport system are nested and connected. Individual departments and roads can be considered as subsystems,

The peculiarity of transport geoinformatics is the use of two types of complex systems: complex data systems and complex technological systems of information processing. One of the primary tasks of transport geoinformatics is to find and formalise spatial relations between transport infrastructure objects. The relations are located in predetermined coordinate systems.

Coordinate systems establish spatial relations between transport infrastructure objects [201], including mobile objects. Relationships and connections are established on the basis of qualitative [202] and quantitative attributes using geometry, spatial logic, set theory, At the same time in geoinformatics different coordinate systems are used, but in a single environment, which allows to move from one to another if necessary. The method of classifications is based on the establishment of spatial relations on the basis of qualitative features between objects and their elements and complements the method of coordinate systems in geoinformatics. Together, both methods provide completeness of analysis.

The peculiarity of the development of transport geoinformatics is that it emerged and develops on the basis of integration of sciences and due to this is a tool for interdisciplinary knowledge transfer. The integration process is based on the system approach, integration of knowledge, finding the unity and integrity of "integrating" disciplines, obtaining the synergetic effect of

integration [203-206].
The methodology of transport geoinformatics is based on the use of information and geoinformation modelling methods to obtain knowledge, models or data used in other disciplines. Information modelling as a fundamental method of cognition [207] makes it possible to compare phenomena based on the use of information models. Information modelling complements and increases the efficiency of using computational tools.
Visual modelling is fully represented in geoinformatics of transport. Geoinformatics includes in the processing and analysis of graphical representation of spatially distributed information, which allows to effectively process and analyse regional information and make a visual comparative analysis of the state of the education system in the subjects of the federation and even at the level of smaller territorial units.
Incorporating remote sensing data into geoinformation technologies allows to promptly monitor all significant changes in the transport sphere and, comparing them with current information, to form more accurate management decisions. Geoinformatics provides a tool for analysing transport networks, supplementing it with a visual one. Thus, transport geoinformatics provides an opportunity to study transport problems in a multidimensional and comprehensive way.
One of the peculiarities of transport geoinformatics is the study of roads and railway tracks of network systems, which on the one hand are a complex system as a complex of structures and devices, on the other hand are specific topological objects. This makes it necessary to use the theory of topology in the study of transport systems using geoinformatics methods.

2.5 Economic Geoinformatics

Economic geoinformatics is a synthesis of geoinformatics and spatial economics. The analysis of management problems, management development trends and the need to apply spatial information justify the need to introduce a new scientific direction "economic geoinformatics". The application of economic geoinformatics increases the efficiency of economic and management decisions. Methodologically, economic geoinformatics requires the introduction of balancing technology of geoinformatics and economic technologies.
The development of geoinformatics has led to the need to introduce the field of economic geoinformatics. Geographic information systems [208, 209] and geographic information technologies are used for management and decision support [210].
Nowadays, there are many types of management that are related to either

spatial information [211] or spatial management [212]. Information management [213] and digital management [214], which is fully aligned with geoinformatics, are intensively developing. The direction of geoinformation management [215-217], which means geoinformation management, has been formed abroad. Corporate management [218-220], which is often related to spatial information and is spatial management, is developing. Logistics is closely related to geoinformatics [221] and spatial economics [222]. Currently, soft management [223, 224] is developing alongside the traditional directive direction. Both types of management are realised by methods of geoinformatics. Real estate management is closely connected with geoinformatics [225-227]. Problems of sustainable development of territories [228], land use support [229], geomarketing [230, 231] and geoservice [232] are realised using geoinformatics. This part of geoinformatics belongs to the field of economic geoinformatics, Geoinformatics has long been used to support economic calculations or directly for calculations. All this makes the research of the field of economic geoinformatics relevant.

The components of economic geoinformatics form a structure. Figure 2.1 shows the structure of economic geoinformatics.

Fig.2.1 Structure of economic geoinformatics.

In Figure 2.1, the dashed line indicates the geoinformatics approach [233, 234]. It is common for different specialisations of geoinformatics. Geoinformational economic modelling uses different types of modelling/ First of all it is geoinformational modelling [235-237]. Spatial modelling [238] serves as the basis of modelling in economic geoinformatics. Economic and mathematical modelling is a mandatory component of economic geoinformatics. Other types of modelling include: information modelling, numerical modelling [239], metamodelling, algorithmic modelling, semasiological modelling [240].

The important components of economic geoinformatics should include monitoring as a tool for obtaining spatial information. econmic information and management information. the basis of many types of monitoring is geoinformation monitoring. Its important complement is economic monitoring [241]. Geotechnical monitoring is used to monitor objects [242]. Information monitoring is used to analyse information.

The place of economic geoinformatics in the system of sciences is shown in Fig. 2.2.

Fig.2.2 Place of economic geoinformatics

Economic geoinformatics is in the system of sciences as an equal among equals. It belongs to the field of specialised areas of geoinformatics. This system is a network structure, which resembles a semantic network. Economic geoinformatics is related to transport geoinformatics, environmental geoinformatics [243], logistics geoinformatics, dynamic geoinformatics [244]. Among economic sciences, economic geoinformatics is primarily related to spatial economics and regional economics [245]. Economic geoinformatics is related to space geoinformatics [] in the aspect of feasibility of space research. Economic geoinformatics finds application in construction, municipal management, land use, in cadastre

The main objectives of economic geoinformatics are: reducing the complexity of management, increasing the efficiency of management using spatial information, and integrating geoinformatics methods with management and economic analysis.

There is an objective reason for the reduction of management efficiency in modern conditions. It is caused by the growing complexity of management with the enlargement of management objects. Complexity reduces the effectiveness of the old management. The enlargement of objects requires the application of new management methods and finding new resources. Another reason for the decrease in management efficiency is the growth of data volumes and the emergence of the big data problem. Spatial information is a resource of real estate management and can create synergetic effect [246]. Therefore, the application of spatial management and geoinformatics increases the efficiency of management.

The emergence and development of economic geoinformatics is a consequence of the modern development of society and the expansion of the application of geoinformatics. The second important reason for the application of economic geoinformatics is the increasing role of spatial factors in management. The increase of management factors is always accompanied by the complication of management. Reducing the complexity of management is due to the creation of new models and new scientific directions. In modern conditions the application of economic geoinformatics is mandatory. In this case, information-computer systems and information-computer networks play a great role. Methodologically, economic geoinformatics requires compliance with the condition of complementarity. Management with the application of economic geoinformatics can be multi-purpose. Geoinformatics management strategy should be coordinated with data structures and information processing technologies. Economic geoinformatics improves the efficiency and effectiveness of management. Economic geoinformatics allows to solve new complex problems that conventional management does not solve.

2.6 Geoinformation-based property management

Real estate management applies spatial information of two types. The first type of spatial information relates to the location of an object in a particular coordinate system. The second type of information describes the dimensions and spatial features of the object. A real estate object is a spatial object. Its size and area affect the value of the object and the management of the object. The processing of spatial information is handled by geoinformatics. Geoinformatics contains management resources [88]. Therefore, its application to real estate management is appropriate [247]. There is a reason to introduce the concept of "geoinformatics-based real estate management" (GIM). A broader concept is geoinformation land management (GILM). Real estate management (REM) is a special scientific direction. It is neighbouring with it corporate real estate management (CREM). The basis of REM is a formal language or a system of information units of management. The peculiarity of REM is cyclicity, including monitoring and step-by-step management. The peculiarity of the real estate state is its dependence on the external environment and the situation of the environment. This requires the consideration of information situation models [248] in real estate management. The information situation can be considered as a condition of management. The state of the real estate object can be associated with the current parametric and spatial situation. Thus, two types of situation and two types of geo-information management can be stated. Management by state parameters and management by spatial state of the object. The spatial aspect becomes especially important in the management of mobile objects and in the management with target selection. For geo-information management of real estate, the abbreviation GREM can be introduced. For GREM there is a concept of management trajectory. A management trajectory is a chain of planned actions. This chain leads the control object from the initial state to the target state. The control trajectory can change due to external factors. GREM has a large number of factors and resources to manage.

GREM features. The general theory of real estate management [249] includes private types of management: corporate real estate management [250 -252], real estate life cycle management [253, 254], real estate operation [255], information support of real estate management, housing management, real estate development [256]. All private types of property management operate in a complementary manner [257]. They apply a harmonised set of concepts and a common terminology, except for Russia. Russia introduces its own terms different from those of European countries. IFMA (International Property Management Association) divides property management into asset, property and facility management. The application of informatics [10], geoinformatics [2, 17] information [84] and geoinformation modelling has influenced the technologies and methods of real estate management. Real estate management is a continuous process of harmonising the needs of users with the changes in the environment and the development trend of society, as well as the development of technology.

The key aspects of property management should be considered as location, value, property function, conjuncture, property quality and property operation quality. The following management components are derived from this: use value, cost, demand, supply, development of real estate utilisation technology. Development of real estate construction technology, development of real estate design technology, development of information modelling technology, development of real estate intellectualisation and intelligent management technology.

The relationship between the buyer of the property and the provider of the built environment plays an important role. A comparison of different property management methods can reveal facts of similarities - differences in management. For example, corporate real estate (CRE) management theories are subsequently placed in the CRE management department within the boundaries of the user organisation. In contrast, housing management theories are most often placed in an industry group outside of households. Current CRE and housing management practice tends towards a portfolio of conventional assets and avoids representative properties such as monuments. There is a tendency for households to want to be more involved and co-produce their home than before and therefore want to bypass the current institutional environment (a kind of insourcing, in-house production). Within organisations there has been a tendency for decades to be less involved in the management of their accommodation and to use the market for related services. Among the objects of individual governance there are objects of corporate governance [258].

Building Information Modelling (BIM) should be highlighted as a modern trend in property management. The emergence of BIM [259] has influenced the mechanism of property management. BIM models embedded in industrial buildings are an important part of the digital transformation of society. The development of executive BIM has enabled property owners to become not only owners of the assets themselves, but also owners of digital assets. Neural networks [260] have been applied in property management. In essence, these models are specialised CAD models or spatial models of specialised GIS.

The widespread growth of information volumes in management and modelling has led to the emergence of the problem of big data and the need to take them into account in real estate management [261]. The development of the economic block of REM is connected with actuarial technologies [262] and forecasting technologies. Geoservices [263] and geomarketing as a technology to support property management are becoming more and more widely used. Geoservice is applied in two qualities. Geoservice is a technology of support and maintenance of real estate. Geoservice is a technology of real estate management support.

Real estate management belongs to the sphere of spatial economy. Therefore, spatial planning is widely used in real estate management. As a modern trend, the contribution of branding theory [252] to corporate property management should be noted. Digital assets play an increasing role in property management [264]. Decision analysis techniques in real estate management processes are improving. They apply multi-criteria analysis [265] to solve the problems of this direction. They use the method of key indicators [266] for property management.

Real estate has different forms of ownership. It can be municipal, sectoral, educational institution-owned and corporate real estate. The diversity of real estate forms creates the complexity of real estate management. General management methods [267], methods of state management of land and property complex [268], methods of commercial management, including real estate management [269] based on key indicators are used for real estate management.

Modern property management requires the application of applied informatics, management information technology [270] and information management. Modern property management requires the application of intelligent management and even cyber-physical technologies. Information monitoring and geoinformation monitoring are applied to collect information for real estate management [271]. Real estate objects are spatial objects. This requires the involvement of spatial management techniques. In addition, spatial geoinformatics is applied in GREM [272]. Real estate management for complex objects uses modelling. For GREM, spatial modelling techniques are applied

The use of GIS and real estate information systems is accompanied by the processing of visual spatial models. This motivates the need for visual representation [273, 274] of spatial management information. In GREM, there is a need for the application of visual property models.

Management information must be stored for later analysis. This requires the use of databases, geodatabases, data warehouses [275], repositories [276]. For sectoral management, spatial data infrastructure [277] must be utilised. Specialised information systems [278] and application systems are used in GREM. Real estate management requires the accumulation, generalisation and use of experience. Metamodelling is applied for this purpose [279, 280].

There is a tendency to use specialised management systems for the management of real estate, especially for the management of state-owned real estate [281]. Public real estate management systems are complex and country-specific, resulting in differences between detailed procedures for managing resource property. Nevertheless, they can be compared in terms of adherence to good governance principles.

The harmonious and sustainable development of modern societies is inseparable from the efficient utilisation of resources to meet the needs of the population. Optimising management by managing resources wisely and protecting the needs of the public is particularly important and challenging from the perspective of sustainable development. Therefore, stakeholders need a new management model for public buildings [282] based on sustainability criteria. There is a relationship between environmental quality, socio-spatial segregation and social aspect of sustainability in urban areas [282]. The relationship between the three dimensions of sustainability (environmental, economic and social) and residential segregation is assessed for urban areas. Multivariate indices of segregation and sustainability are created using data aggregated by Census Core-Based Statistical Areas CBSA. The relationship between segregation and resilience (and size independently) is analysed within the CBSA using correlation and spatial analyses. The results of [283] show an inverse relationship between segregation and sustainability, where an increase in urban segregation corresponds to a decrease in sustainability. The social and economic aspects of sustainability are negatively correlated with segregation, while the environmental aspect has a positive correlation. These correlations point to the need to consider inequality and social aspects of sustainability more broadly in property management planning.

Real estate management of dual-subordination industry objects comes from two management centres [284]. The industry management centre and the enterprise centre. This leads to possible conflicts of management. For such management the factor of coordination of management from two centres is important. For such management it is necessary to apply industry GIS or situation centres.

Geoinformation property management belongs to the field of spatial economics and is a new property management technology. GREM uses general and specialised management technologies. GREM is a more complex type of management in comparison with parametric property management. GREM solves economic and social problems. The trend of emergence and development of "smart cities" also influences property management technologies and GREM. Smart cities are considered as complex technological systems or as complex organisational and technical systems. Overcoming organisational challenges in smart cities is done through collective action, including corporate property management. Assessing the environmental, social and economic performance of building upgrades for different types of buildings and housing models also becomes an important factor in property management. Property management is a complex technological and scientific complex that solves a variety of problems. It requires the development of these theories and technologies.

CHAPTER 3

3. Information gathering in applied geoinformatics

3.1. General approaches to information collection

Information is collected to fulfil information needs [285]. Information collection technologies collect information about objects on the basis of direct and indirect measurements. The main technologies of spatial information collection include: geodetic, photogrammetric, cartographic, space, statistical technologies (Fig. 3.1) and satellite technologies.

Fig.3.1 Main data collection technologies in applied geoinformatics.

Geodetic, photogrammetric, cartographic, space information collection technologies collect spatial information. Statistical information has different nature and is not originally spatial. Therefore in the process of collection localisation or binding of statistical information to spatial information is carried out. Characteristic for information collection technologies in geoinformatics is the storage of collected information in different systems: in information system (IS), in geographic information system (GIS), database (DB), spatial database (SDB), geodatabase (GDD), spatial data infrastructure (SDI).

Primary sources of spatial information can be objects of the surrounding world. Secondary sources of information can be databases, archives and network resources. The collected information is registered, coded, annotated, systematised and unified. Automated registration is performed without human participation and involves direct connection of the information and measurement system [286] to the measurements. The collected information contains primary data.

Primary data are data that capture the parameters being measured. The fixation of parameters consists in their description by means of quantitative and qualitative quantities. These quantities may contain errors and anomalous errors due to failures. Therefore, during the processing of primary information it is necessary to identify and eliminate anomalous measurements [287]. o leads to the need to use measurement scales. To ensure comparability of measurements, the principle of unity of measurements is used.

3.2. Unity of measurement

Unity of measurements is an important condition that ensures comparability of measurement results and the possibility of their joint use for analysing and solving practical problems. All characteristics of geoinformatics research objects have qualitative and quantitative values. For example, 10 mm, 10 m and 10 km have the same quantitative values, but different scales, i.e. different qualities within the measured parameter - distance.

The values: velocity 10 m/sec, distance 10 m, acceleration 10 m/(sec)^2 - also have the same quantitative values, but describe qualitatively different parameters. Thus, only quantitative values do not allow to compare the parameters, qualitative correspondence is also necessary. The principle of unity of measurement serves as the basis for such correspondence.

Unity of measurements is a state of measurements, at which their results are expressed in standardised units of quantities and measurement errors do not exceed the established limits with a given probability. This definition is given by the Law of the Russian Federation "On Ensuring Uniformity of Measurements". Unity of measurements is necessary in order to be able to compare the results of measurements performed in different places and at different times, using different methods and measuring instruments.

The content of the concept of "unity of measurement" is rather capacious. It covers the most important tasks of metrology: unification of units, development of systems for reproduction of units and transfer of their dimensions to working measuring instruments with established accuracy, carrying out measurements with an error not exceeding the established limits, etc. The unity of measurement should be maintained at any accuracy of measurements. Unity of measurements shall be maintained at any accuracy of measurements. Within the framework of ensuring the uniformity of measurements the following basic concepts shall be applied:

unity of measurements - the state of measurements, at which their results are expressed in legalised units of quantities and measurement errors do not exceed the established limits with a given probability;

measuring instrument - a technical device intended for measurement;

unit standard - measuring instrument intended for reproduction and storage of a unit (or multiples or fractions of a unit) for the purpose of transferring its size to other measuring instruments of the given unit;

state standard of a unit of magnitude - a standard of a unit of magnitude recognised by the decision of an authorised state body as a reference standard on the territory of the Russian Federation;
normative documents on ensuring the uniformity of measurements - state standards, international (regional) standards, rules, regulations, instructions and recommendations applied in accordance with the established procedure;
verification of a measuring instrument - a set of operations performed by state metrological service bodies (other authorised bodies, organisations) in order to determine and confirm the conformity of a measuring instrument to the established technical requirements;
calibration of a measuring instrument - a set of operations performed in order to determine and confirm the actual values of metrological characteristics and (or) suitability for use of a measuring instrument not subject to state metrological control and supervision;
certificate of approval of type of measuring instruments - a document issued by the authorised state body certifying that the given type of measuring instruments is approved in accordance with the procedure stipulated by the current legislation and complies with the established requirements;
licence for manufacturing (repair, sale, rental) of measuring instruments - a document certifying the right to engage in the specified activities, issued to legal entities and individuals by the state metrological service body;
calibration certificate - a document certifying the fact and results of calibration of a measuring instrument, which is issued by the organisation performing the calibration.

Measuring instruments subject to state metrological control and supervision shall be subject to *verification* by the bodies of the State Metrological Service at release from production or repair, at importation and operation. Only verified measuring instruments may be sold and hired out.

Lists of groups of measuring instruments subject to verification shall be approved by Gosstandart of Russia. Unity of measurements makes the results of measurements practically usable. On the contrary, violation of the principle of unity of measurements makes the results unsuitable for use, both in theory and in practice.

3.3. Geodetic technologies for information gathering

Fig. 3.2. shows the scheme of information collection with the help of geodetic methods. This group of technologies uses different approaches and instruments. It uses ground-based manual and automated surveying instruments. The main range of information acquisition in this group of technologies is the optical range.

Geodetic measurements - measurements carried out with the help of geodetic instruments, according to special technologies and methods. Initially collected information is called primary information and requires primary processing, equalisation and unification. Primary information is converted into geodata for subsequent modelling processing.

Fig.3.2 Geodetic technologies of spatial information acquisition in geoinformatics

Geodetic measurements can be made not only on the surface of the Earth, but also on any other celestial body.

There are different areas and types of geodetic measurements. *Area of geodetic measurements* - classification category of geodetic measurements, distinguished on the basis of their purpose. The following areas of geodetic measurements are distinguished: *Basis* measurements - area of geodetic measurements related to the determination of lengths of bases (or their intervals). *Astronomical-geodetic measurements* - area of geodetic measurements related to the determination of astronomical and geodetic coordinates. *Levelling* - area of geodetic measurements related to the determination of heights (height differences).

Geodynamic measurements - the field of geodetic measurements related to the determination of changes in the position of geodetic points in time relative to the accepted starting points, as well as the interpretation of the obtained results.

Stem measurements - the area of geodetic measurements related to the determination of deviations of the position of points (points) from a straight line (a given stem).

Topographic survey - a field of geodetic measurements related to the creation of a plan (map) of an object, carried out at the object of measurement in combination with the collection and analysis of information.

Type of geodetic measurements - a classification category of geodetic measurements, distinguished on the basis of the measured geodetic quantity. The following types of geodetic measurements are distinguished:

Angular (geodetic) measurements - type of geodetic measurements in which the measured geodetic quantity is horizontal and (or) vertical angles (zenith distances).

Linear (geodetic) measurements - a type of geodetic measurements in which the measured geodetic quantity is the lengths of the sides of geodetic networks (distances or their differences).

Geodetic elevation measurements - a type of linear geodetic measurements, in which the measured geodetic quantity is the difference of heights of points (points).

Gyroscopic measurements (gyroscopic orientation) - a type of angular geodetic measurements, in which the measured geodetic quantity is the azimuths of directions determined with the help of gyroscopic instruments.

Geodetic coordinate measurements (coordinate measurements) - a type of geodetic measurements in which the measured geodetic quantity is the position of geodetic points relative to the reference points in a given reference system.

3.4. Geodetic networks

Geodetic networks fulfil two main tasks: creating a unified coordinate environment; supporting measurements and coordinate transformation. They provide unity of geodetic and other spatial measurements within the state. In addition, networks allow to work in local coordinate systems without being bound to a single coordinate system. Binding (transition) to a unified coordinate system of the state is carried out by binding to a point of the network. This allows to bring the measurement results to the geocentric system or other national system

Geodetic *network* (Geodetic net) - A network of fixed points of the Earth's surface, whose position is defined in a common system of geodetic coordinates. There are quite a large number of networks. All geodetic networks can be divided according to the following features. By *territorial* feature: global, state geodetic networks (GGS), special purpose networks (GSSN), survey networks. By *geometric nature of* networks are divided into: planned, height, spatial networks.

Global networks are created for the whole surface of the Earth by satellite methods, being spatial with the origin of coordinates in the centre of mass of the Earth and defined in the coordinate system PZ-90

National networks are divided into: State Geodetic Network (GGS) in Gauss-Kruger projection on the plane and the State Leveling Network (SLN) with definition of normal heights in the Baltic system, i.e. from the zero of the Kronstadt Footstock.

Special purpose geodetic networks (SPGN) are created when further densification of GGS points is not economically feasible or when a particularly high accuracy of the geodetic network is required. Depending on the purpose, these networks can be plan, height, plan-altitude and even spatial and can be created in any coordinate system.

Survey grids are the justification for various local works and are usually created by plan-levelling grids.

State geodetic network (SGS) is a system of points fixed on the ground, the position of which is defined in a unified system of coordinates and heights, legally adopted in a given state. The GGS is designed to solve the following main tasks of economic, scientific and defence importance:

- establishment and dissemination of a unified state system of geodetic coordinates throughout the country and its maintenance at the level of modern and prospective requirements;
- geodetic support for mapping the territory of Russia and the waters of the surrounding seas;
- geodetic support for the study of land resources and land use, cadastre, construction, exploration and development of natural resources;
- providing initial geodetic data for land, marine and aerospace navigation, aerospace monitoring of natural and man-made environments;
- study of the Earth's surface and gravitational field and their changes in time;
- the study of geodynamic phenomena;
- metrological support of high-precision technical means of positioning and orientation.

Geodetic heights of GGS points are determined as the sum of normal and quasigeoid heights above the reference ellipsoid either directly by space geodesy methods or by referencing to points with known geocentric coordinates. The normal heights of GGS points are defined in the Baltic Height System 1977, the initial origin of which is the zero of the Kronstadt Footstick. The GGS scale is set by the Unified State Standard of time-frequency-length. In works on the development of GGS the scales of atomic TA (SU) and coordinated UTC (SU) time set by the existing standard base of the Russian

Federation are used, as well as the Earth rotation parameters and corrections for transition to international time scales, periodically published by Gosstandart of Russia in special bulletins of the State Time and Frequency Service (STFS).

Astronomical latitudes and longitudes, astronomical and geodetic azimuths determined from observations of stars are brought to the system of the fundamental star catalogue, to the system of the mean pole and to the system of astronomical longitudes adopted at the epoch of GGS equalisation.

Metrological support of geodetic works is carried out in accordance with the requirements of the State System for Ensuring Uniformity of Measurements.

GGS combines a number of networks into one whole:

astronomical-geodetic points of the space geodetic network (SGN AGP),

Doppler geodetic network (DGS),

astronomical-geodetic network (ATS) of classes 1 and 2,

geodetic densification networks (GDS) of classes 3 and 4,

The GGS is structured according to the principle of transition from general to particular and includes geodetic constructions of different accuracy classes: fundamental astronomical-geodetic network (FAGS), high-precision geodetic network (HGN), satellite geodetic network of the 1st class (GGS-1).

The existing triangulation and polygonometry networks of classes 1-4 are also included in the above system of constructions. Permanent differential stations are created on the basis of new high-precision points of the satellite network in order to ensure the possibility of coordinates determination by consumers in near-real time mode.

As the FAGS, GGS and GGS-1 networks are being developed, the GGS is being equalised and the parameters of mutual orientation of the geocentric coordinate system and the SK-95 geodetic coordinate system are being specified. The density of GGS points on a scale of 1 point per: average distance:

1:25000 50-60 km^2 7-8 km

1:10000 50-60 km^2 7-8 km

1:5000 20-30 km^2 5-6 km

1:2000 5-15 km^2 2-4 km

Length error: ms = 0.25 *pM,*

where ts is the graphical length error on the map, *M* is the denominator of the scale.

At each point of the existing GGS in accordance with the "Instruction on the construction of the state geodetic network", are determined by two landmark points with underground centres, numbered from the direction north clockwise, at a distance from the centre of the point of at least 500 m in the open and 250 m in the inscribed area, with visibility to them directly from the centre.

The heights of all GGS points are determined mainly by trigonometric levelling on the sides of the network from points taken as reference points, which are determined by geometric levelling and are located at least 3 sides of the polygonometry or 75 km in the triangulation network.

Reference geodetic network is a network or system of points selected and fixed in a certain way on the terrain, which serve as reference points during topographic surveying and geodetic measurements on the terrain. Reference geodetic network is of great practical importance for drawing topographic maps, determining the shape and size of the Earth. There is a distinction between plan and height reference geodetic networks. Planned reference geodetic network is created mainly by triangulation, and the mutual position of its points is determined by geodetic coordinates or, more often, rectangular coordinates. High-altitude reference geodetic network (levelling network) is created by the method of geometric levelling, by means of which the elevations of points above sea level are determined. For example, a boundary reference network (BRN) is used to solve boundary surveying tasks.

3.5. Photogrammetric technologies of spatial information acquisition

Fig. 3.4 shows the scheme of collection technologies with the help of photogrammetric technologies. The main range of information acquisition in this group of technologies is optical range. In geodetic technologies information collection is carried out on point-by-point basis. Photogrammetric technologies collect information on terrain fragments by a group of points on images.

The peculiarity of photogrammetric technologies, as well as geodetic technologies, is that on the one hand they serve as a basis for information collection in geoinformatics, and on the other hand they carry out independent processing and production. Therefore, it is difficult to distinguish pure collection in photogrammetric and geodetic technologies. It is necessary to consider these technologies comprehensively

Modern photogrammetry uses many types of images obtained with cameras, digital cameras, television cameras, scanner survey systems, radar and mobile laser scanning systems, etc. There are three main directions in photogrammetry. The first direction is related to creation of maps and plans based on images. This direction is often called phototopography. The second direction of photogrammetry application is connected with solution of applied tasks. This direction is called applied photogrammetry. Applied photogrammetry is used in architecture, construction, land cadastre, land monitoring, monitoring of precipitation and deformation of structures, medicine, forensics, automotive industry, robotics, military, geology, etc. The third direction related to obtaining information from space carriers is called space photogrammetry.

According to the methods of obtaining information, the following types of this technology are distinguished: space photogrammetry, aerial photogrammetry (airborne), ground photogrammetry. According to the methods of information processing the following types of this technology are distinguished: analytical photogrammetry, analogue photogrammetry, digital. The technologies of photogrammetric information processing are shown in Fig.3.4. They include monoscopic and stereoscopic methods. All technologies are based on image processing.

Fig.3.4 Photogrammetric information processing technologies

Processing results are reduced to obtaining coordinates of object points and building models. Photogrammetric methods are used for construction of digital models (DM), digital elevation models (DEM), digital maps (DM), photomaps, photo schemes, orthophoto plans and other products. Image processing is preceded by photo interpretation, i.e. a technology of photo pre-processing in order to recognise objects depicted on them, to determine their qualitative and quantitative characteristics and to select objects, if necessary.

The result of photogrammetric processing can be not only catalogues of

coordinates, but also cartographic products and special types of products, such as photogrammetric scheme and photoplane.
A photogram is a photographic image of terrain obtained by assembling useful areas of untransformed plan aerial images by their common points or by their initial directions. Production of a photomap does not require field preparation and transformation of aerial images, therefore it can be obtained in a short period of time after aerial survey. The photomap is used to study the terrain for surveys that do not require precise measurements. The scale of the photomap is equal to the scale of the aerial photograph. A photomontage mounted along the initial directions is slightly more accurate than one mounted along the contours and is called a refined photomontage, but it takes more time to produce than an ordinary photomontage.
Photoplane is a photographic image of the terrain obtained as a result of assembly of useful areas of transformed aerial photographs by reference points. A photoplane is usually produced within the survey trapezoid; the accuracy of contours position relative to geodetic points corresponds to the accuracy of a topographic map of the same scale as the photoplane. Reproductions from a photoplane are used for drawing reliefs on them during topographic surveying and as an independent document during surveying and construction works requiring detailed study of the terrain and accurate determination of distances or areas

3.6. Cartographic technologies for the collection of spatial information

Fig. 3.5. shows the scheme of information acquisition using cartographic information. The main range of information collection in this group of technologies is the optical range. The initial basis is paper maps, which are converted into digital maps.

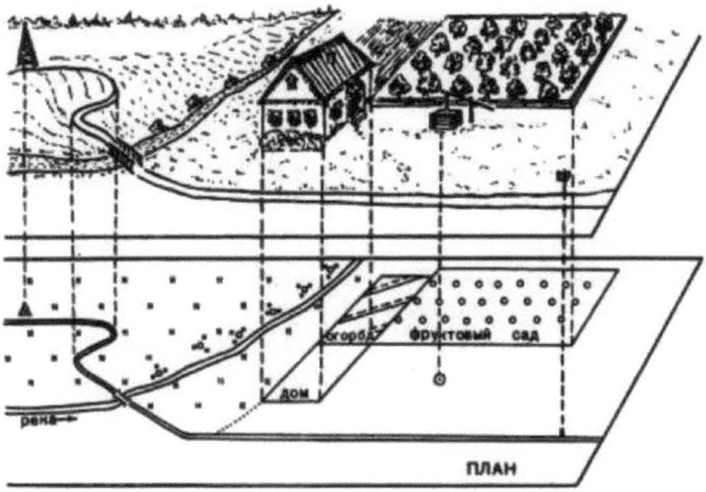

Figure 3.5: Cartographic technologies for spatial information collection

It should be remembered that a map is a flat two-dimensional model of a three-dimensional non-planar object (the Earth's surface). It always contains cartographic distortions that three-dimensional digital models do not. A topographic map and a topographic plan are a reduced image on a plane of terrain areas, but there are significant differences between them. The scale within a plan is constant. On small and medium scale maps, the scale changes from point to point and in directions. The scale established for a given map is observed only in one of the directions (one meridian or parallel), this scale is called the main scale. In other parts of the map the scales differ from the main scale and are called private scales.

The semiotic aspect allows us to consider the map as a figurative-sign model. The content of topographic maps is expressed by topographic symbols. The maps show: hydrographic network and natural formations attached to it (shoals, ice, etc.), groundwater outlets, surface relief - with horizontals, height marks and additional designations (for cliffs, berms, scour holes, etc.). The topographic maps show vegetation with subdivision according to the cover closure. They show soils, glaciers and snowfields, bogs and solonchaks with demonstration of their passability, main agricultural lands, settlements with transfer of their structure and type (city, working settlement, etc.).

Map nomenclature is a system for designating individual sheets of a multi-sheet map. By international agreement, the nomenclature of map sheets at a scale of 1: 1,000,000 is uniform for all countries. For maps at other scales, the nomenclature may vary from country to country

For topographic maps, an *alphanumeric coding of* sheets, ordered by scale, is introduced. This defines nomenclature as a natural hierarchical classification. The basis of classification is a map of scale 1:1000000. The system of dividing maps into sheets is called *rasgraphy.*

The curvilinear part of the Earth's surface displayed on a map sheet corresponds to a curvilinear trapezoid. The curvilinearity of a trapezoid is caused by the division of the Earth's surface by meridians and parallels, which define such curvilinear trapezoids. Each sheet of a topographic map is a trapezoid bounded by the straightened arcs of meridians and parallels, the size of which is determined by the map scale and latitude of the terrain. Therefore, the term trapezoid is used to refer to certain map sheets.

The nomenclature of maps at different scales is based on the international map layout at a scale of 1: 1,000,000. To obtain one sheet of a map of this scale, the entire globe is divided by meridians from the Greenwich meridian through 6° in longitude into 60 columns (bicolumns). The bicolumns are numbered with Arabic numerals from 1 to 60 east of 180°. Numbering from 0° is possible. In this case, the bipeds are not called columns, but zones. The numbering of zones differs from columns by 30 units, for example, a column with number 40 corresponds to a zone with number 10

Thus, the number of columns differs from the number of the 6° zone by 30. Each column is divided by parallels through 4° of latitude into rows, designated by capital letters of the Latin alphabet, north and south of the equator. Thus, the entire surface of the globe is depicted on 2640 sheets. All of the above properties of maps also apply to digital maps

3.7. Collection of information using remotely sensed data from the Earth

Fig. 3.6. shows a scheme of collection technologies using space-based methods or remotely sensed data. This group of technologies is heterogeneous, because unlike the previous groups, collection is carried out in different bands: optical, infrared, radar and even X-ray. To eliminate heterogeneity, an additional step "harmonisation of data from different bands" is included in the collection technology.

In the modern world, the space industry is one of the most priority and knowledge-intensive areas of human activity. Participation in space activities largely determines the political prestige of a modern state, its economic, scientific, technological and defence power. The advantage of remote sensing methods in relation to ground and air observation methods is the simultaneous acquisition of information on large territories and remote objects, as well as to study the dynamics of spatial objects in different periods of time.

In a broad sense, remote sensing (RS) is the acquisition by any non-contact methods of information about objects on the Earth's surface or in its interior. These methods are used by photogrammetry, geodesy, optics, physics, and radio engineering.

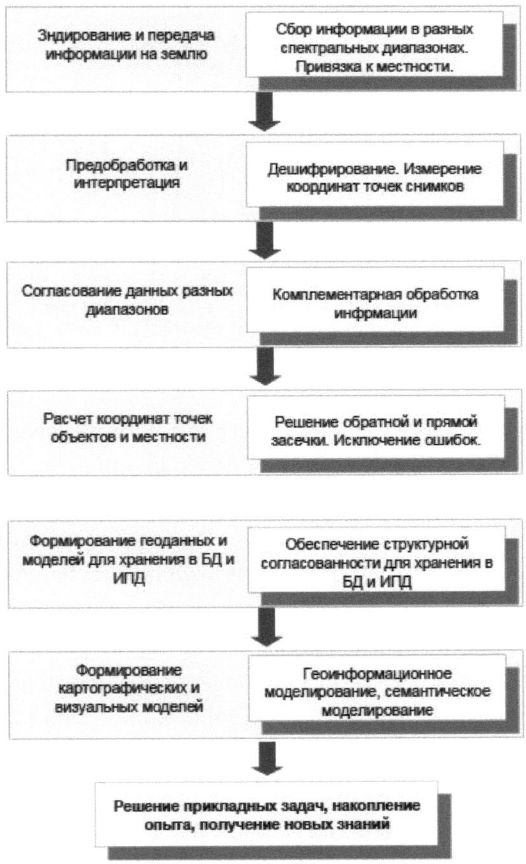

Figure 3.6: Gathering spatial information in geoinformatics using remote sensing techniques

In a narrow sense, remote sensing of the Earth is the acquisition of information using equipment installed on board spacecraft. Remote sensing data (RSD) is the main source for maintaining up-to-date information on objects and processes on the Earth's surface. Their acquisition is summarised in Fig. 3.7

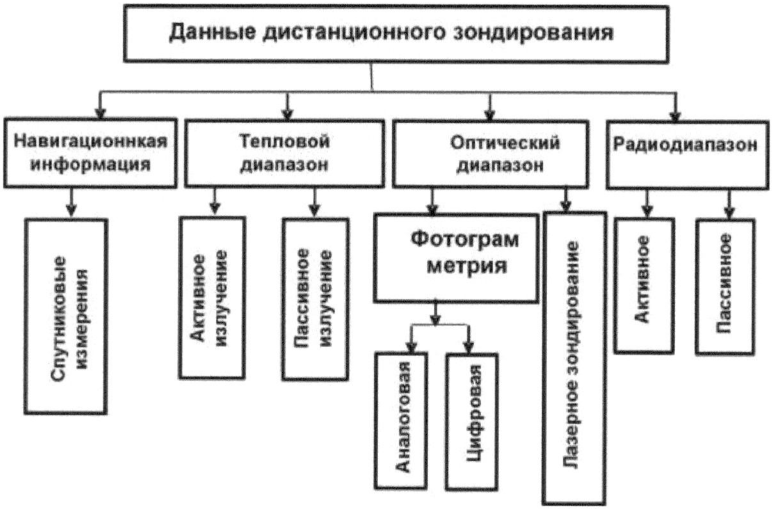

Figure 3.7: Acquisition and application of remotely sensed Earth observation data

Remote sensing methods are characterised by the fact that the recording device is significantly distant from the object under investigation. Distance is an important parameter that determines the distance of the survey instrument from the object of observation. Distance affects the accuracy of measurements. In remote surveys it is possible to obtain information about the object of study in different spectral ranges: X-ray, ultraviolet, visible, infrared. The shorter the wavelength, the higher the accuracy of measuring the position of the object. Optical wavelengths are shorter than thermal or radar wavelengths. Therefore, optical observations recorded on photographic film or with scanning devices are more informative and accurate. The complexity of remote sensing technologies is determined by the significant influence of interference on the useful signal.

Space imaging - imaging of the Earth and celestial bodies by equipment located outside the Earth's atmosphere and providing images in various areas of the electromagnetic spectrum.

Difference between aerial and space photography. The flying heights of aerial photography are much lower than those of space photography. In space studies of phenomena and processes on the Earth's surface, distances to objects can vary from hundreds to thousands of kilometres. One space image can cover an area covered by up to 1000 aerial images Space images create a maximum view of the surface and allow obtaining generalised images.

The trajectory of an airborne vehicle can undergo significant shifts due to wind, air pits, turbulence, etc. The trajectory of a space launch vehicle is close to a mathematical curve

3.8. Collection of information using satellite technology

At present, a new method of information collection using Global Navigation Satellite Systems (GNSS) is widely used [288-290]. In this method, special satellite receivers are used, with the help of which spatial coordinates can be determined at any point of the Earth's surface, which is within the range of GNSS satellites. When using satellite measurements, the coordinates are obtained at any point in space, that is, continuously, which corresponds to the concept of information field [291-293]. The satellite method defines a geoinformation field as a spatial field, at each point of which three coordinates can be calculated. The geoinformation field creates the possibility of determining coordinates at a point in the field and the possibility of evaluating spatial relations in the spatial information situation. Satellite measurements are linked to a special network to increase accuracy, but the measurements are also carried out continuously and with greater accuracy.

Currently, two satellite-based positioning systems are mainly used: the Russian GLONASS system and the American NAVSTAR GPS system. Originally, the systems were created to solve military tasks, but then, with certain limitations, they found application in civilian projects.

The systems provide the determination of coordinate increments with a mean square error of 2 mm+2-10^{-7} D, where *D is the* distance between satellite receivers, and the coordinates of a single receiver can be determined with a mean square error of 3 to 5 metres.

Global Navigation Satellite Systems contain three segments: space (satellites), ground (monitoring and control stations) and user (satellite signal receivers) [294]. The essence of creating a geoinformation or navigation field is to use GNSS and computational processing system to obtain coordinates.

The location of a point in a geoinformation field can be obtained using absolute [294] and relative [294] measurements. Absolute determinations use the measurement of the receiver location relative to four satellites in orbits. Absolute determinations (less accurate) are made on the principle of spatial backtracking, formed by measured pseudo-distances to 4 or more satellites from a definable point on which the satellite receiver is placed. The standard accuracy of positioning by the absolute method can reach 3-5 metres, and such accuracy does not allow the method to be used for many tasks. This is due to the long distance to the satellites.

The relative or differential measurement method is based on relative (more accurate) measurements. At least two receivers are used. One receiver is permanently installed at a point with known coordinates. It is called a reference station or base station (BS) [295]. The second receiver (mobile station - MS) is located at the point in the navigation field whose coordinates are to be determined.

The method is applicable only in the BS coverage area. It should be called situational, since it also depends on the modes of operation, i.e. on the specific information situation. In this connection, it is necessary to introduce the concept of "observation zone" as an area in which it is possible to obtain coordinates of points using satellite equipment relative to the BS. The following methods of relative satellite determinations are distinguished:

Static (static) [296]- a method in which synchronous observations on the BS and MS are performed in one go for at least 30-60 minutes;

Fast static (fast static) [297] - a method in which synchronous observations at the base station and mobile station located at the point to be determined are performed in a single acquisition lasting 5-20 minutes. The observation time depends on the number of observed satellites.

Kinematic method [298], in which one receiver operates on the BS and the second receiver on the MS is in continuous operation while travelling between field points.

The initial stage of work on coordinate measurement is determination of BS coordinates. To determine the coordinates of the BS, the points of the network (geodetic base), which are located within the observation area, are usually used.

It is recommended to use all points of the state geodetic network (GGS). In this case, if points are different, then use at least 4 points with known plan coordinates and at least 5 points with known heights, in order to ensure that the plan-altitude justification is brought into the system of coordinates and heights of points of the geodetic basis for determining the position of the BS.

It is recommended to use the construction of a network of triangulation methods to determine the position of the BS [299]. The locations of BSs are chosen taking into account their clear observation by GNSS. A distinction is made between "good" and "bad" BS locations. A good BS location has the following characteristics:

no obstacles to measurements between the BS and MS at angles above 15 degrees above the horizon;

No parasitic reflective surfaces that create interference or radio echoes;

MC installation sites are away from moving traffic and from casual passers-by;

Powerful radio transmitters and other systems that create radio interference must not be located in the observation area.

It is preferable to organise temporary BSs at sites that fully meet the above requirements. In practice, BSs are often located on the roofs of buildings or on capital walls.

The accuracy of the BS installation sets the accuracy of the MS measurements. Therefore, the static method of satellite observations is chosen to determine the coordinates of the BS. At all points of the geodetic base, participating in the determination of the "base", the satellite observation session lasts at least 60 minutes. The observation time required for Static measurements depends on a number of factors. Static measurement technology is typically used for projects requiring greater accuracy.

After the BS is installed, measurements are made with the MS at periods of time called "observation sessions". A reconnaissance survey should be carried out beforehand to select the points at which the MS is installed. Several sessions may be carried out during the measurement.

Upon completion of satellite measurements, computational processing of satellite observation data is performed. Computational processing is performed by stages: preliminary processing - obtaining coordinate increments from the reference to the points to be determined in the coordinate system of the global navigation satellite system and accuracy assessment; transformation of coordinates of the points to be determined into the local (local) coordinate system; geodetic constructions equalisation and accuracy assessment. At satellite measurements the rule of organisation of cross-control of measurements at the expense of independent measurements is applied. For objective and independent control it is necessary to:

- set the MS to the measurement point for the second time in another observation session;
- close the traverse with a baseline connecting the last observation point with the starting point;
- make independent measurements between points in such a network.

Alternative control can also be performed by the "double measurement method" - using two BSs instead of one. In such double measurements two values of spatial coordinates will be obtained for each MS point. The method of double measurements gives the possibility to use redundant measurements, which provide an additional estimate of the accuracy of the measurement results.

The necessary condition for completion of measurements is transformation of

coordinates of defined points with the help of MS into local (local) coordinate system. The problem of coordinate transformation always arises when a specialist changes reference points when changing the region of works. It is connected with the fact that coordinates of GGS or local coordinate system (LCS) points have errors in centimetres and more. There is no single key to ensure accurate transformation of coordinates. The geodesist has to work in those coordinates, which are stored by points located in the region of works.
The term "geoinformation field" is relatively new and is dictated by the properties of geoinformatics to combine: geodetic, photogrammetric, satellite - observations and observations of mobile laser scanning. Creation of a geoinformation field in this technology consists in creation of a system of base stations, which increases the accuracy of determining the coordinates of this field. The most favourable place for laying the centres of the base station system is the outcrop of bedrock. In cities and towns in the area of seasonal ground freezing the centres are laid on buildings. In the main load-bearing elements of brick, stone, concrete and reinforced concrete buildings and structures built not less than 7 years before the centres of FAGS and VGS points were laid and not less than 3 years before the centres of GHS-1 points were laid. Buildings and structures in which the centres are laid must not have cracks in the walls and visible foundation failures.

CHAPTER 4

4. Coordinate systems in geoinformatics

The principle of unity of measurement requires measurements in a single system for comparison of measurement results. This determines the use of coordinate systems, which are used in photogrammetry, geodesy and geoinformatics. To determine the spatial position of objects of study in geoinformatics, coordinates are used in a pre-selected system.

Different coordinate systems are used in geoinformatics: Cartesian, cylindrical, spherical. Curvilinear coordinates are used on convex surfaces. Adaptability of coordinate systems in geoinformatics is expressed in the possibility of coordinate transformation from one system to another. All existing coordinate systems create the possibility of specifying relations in these systems. Any object that falls into a coordinate system, falls into the system of relations existing in it.

4.1. Basic functions of coordinate systems

Quite often only measuring functions are associated with coordinate systems. However, these functions are secondary. The primary functions are the functions of ordering and finding relations. In this connection it is necessary to recall some terms.

Coordination (from Latin *co* - together and *ordinatio* - ordering), interrelation, coordination, bringing into conformity. The coordinates of a point in the Cartesian rectangular coordinate system are defined as a direct or Cartesian product.

The direct product of three (or *n*) sets A_3 , A_2 , A_3 is defined by *a* tuple of ordered triples $ai*a_2$ $*a_3$. If the sets are non-overlapping and define a space, then the direct product establishes a one-to-one correspondence between the three-dimensional space and the triple of numbers a_3 , a_2 , a_3 .

Coordinates (in geodesy) - values determining the position of a point of the Earth's surface relative to the surface of the Earth's ellipsoid: latitude, longitude, height. They are determined by geodetic methods. Coordinate systems in geoinformatics solve the following functions.

Arrange objects in the chosen system and relative to each other.

Create a one-to-one correspondence between points in space and coordinate parameters.

Enable the realisation of measuring geometric functions.

Enable mathematical transformation of surfaces, lines, spatial objects.

Create an opportunity to realise the functions of relationships (more - less, further - closer)

Enable integration of a variety of information based on georeferencing to

points in space.
Enable you to perform calculations and quantitative analyses.

4.2. Basis coordinate systems.

The basic coordinate systems in geoinformatics are: curvilinear coordinate system, Cartesian coordinate system, cylindrical coordinate system, spherical coordinate system, plane coordinate systems.

Coordinate systems set the information space, so they are not related neither to the shape, nor to the gravity potential, nor to any anomalies or characteristics - of any celestial body.

The content of the space is set by the fields.

Curvilinear coordinate system. In the general case for three-dimensional space, the coordinate system is defined in a curvilinear system by means of coordinate parameters $q1$, q_2, q_3 of three coordinate surfaces

$$q_1 = \varphi_1 (x, y, z), q_2 = \varphi_2 (x, y, z), q_3 = \varphi_3 (x, y, z).$$

Coordinate lines are mutual intersections of coordinate surfaces. In general, these lines are curvilinear, which defines the name of the system as a *curvilinear* coordinate system.

Along the coordinate line of intersection of surfaces, for example, the first and the second, the parameters qi and q_2 remain constant, only the parameter q changes$_3$. Similarly, on the coordinate line of intersection of surfaces two and three, only parameter $q1$ changes, and on the coordinate line of intersection of three and one, only parameter q .$_2$

The origin of the coordinate system e is defined by the intersection point of all three surfaces. Thus, an obligatory condition for specifying the coordinate system by means of the surfaces to be chosen is their intersection at a common point. In the simplest case the surfaces can be planes. If three planes are mutually perpendicular, we come to the Cartesian coordinate system. In the coordinate system there are special lines called coordinate axes. In general, coordinate axes and coordinate lines do not coincide.

Coordinate axes are tangent lines at the point under consideration to the coordinate lines, and the positive directions of these axes are those in the direction of which the changing parameter increases. Curvilinear coordinate systems for which the coordinate axes are mutually perpendicular are called orthogonal. Curvilinear systems are widely used in cartographic projection transformations. The most used in geoinformatics are *rectangular*, *cylindrical* and *spherical* coordinate systems

Rectangular Cartesian coordinate system. In the Cartesian coordinate system, the equations of coordinate surfaces have the form.

$$q_1 = x;\ q_2 = y;\ q_3 = z.$$

Coordinate surfaces are planes mutually perpendicular to each other

$$x = const;\ y = const;\ z = const.$$

Coordinate lines are intersections of planes, i.e. straight lines. The coordinate lines coincide with the coordinate axes. The coordinate axes of this system are mutually perpendicular, so this coordinate system is called orthogonal. The position of a point M in space is determined by specifying its three coordinates M (x; y; z). Special names are used for Cartesian coordinates: **ABSCISSA**, ORDINATA, APPLICATA.

Abscissa (from Latin *abscissa* - cut off), one of the Cartesian coordinates of a point, usually the first, denoted by the letter x.

Ordinate (from Latin *ordinatus* - arranged in order), one of the Cartesian coordinates of a point, usually the second, denoted by the letter y

APPLICATE (from Latin *applicata*, lit. - applied), one of the Cartesian coordinates of a point in space, usually the third, denoted by the letter *z*

Cylindrical coordinate system. In the cylindrical coordinate system, the position of the point *M* in space is determined by specifying the radius-vector - p, the angle of its rotation in the horizontal plane - φ and the applicatio *z*. In the cylindrical coordinate system the equations of surfaces have the form.

$$q_1 = \rho;\ q_2 = \varphi;\ q_3 = z.$$

Connection with rectangular coordinates is carried out by formulas

$$x = \rho \cos \varphi;\ y = \rho \sin \varphi;\ z = z$$

The coordinate surfaces of the cylindrical system are

p = *const* cylinders with axis *Oz;*

φ = *const* half-planes bounded by the *Oz* axis;

z=const planes perpendicular to the *Oz* axis.

Spherical coordinate system. In the spherical coordinate system the position of the point *M* in space is determined by specifying the radius-vector - *r*, its rotation angle in the horizontal plane - f and its rotation angle in the vertical plane θ. In the spherical coordinate system the equations of surfaces are of the form.

$$q_1 = r;\ q_2 = \theta;\ q_3 = \varphi.$$

Connection with rectangular coordinates is carried out by formulas

$$x = r \sin \theta \cos \varphi;\ y = r \sin \theta \sin \varphi;\ z = r \cos \theta$$

The coordinate surfaces of *the* spherical system are *r* = *const* - spheres with centre *O;*

θ =*const* - of the half-plane with the *Oz* axis;

φ =*const* - half-planes bounded by the *Oz* axis.

The importance of spherical coordinate surfaces should be emphasised. If one of the spheres is chosen as a base sphere, then the exceeding or decreasing of the radius of other spheres can be considered as height or depth, relative to the base sphere. This is the model of height measurement adopted for measuring heights on the Earth's surface. This coordinate model makes it possible to create a flat model of a spherical surface.

On a spherical surface, for a sphere of fixed radius, the position of a point is given by the two parameters 0 = *const;* f = *const.* The two parameters of the curved surface can be related to the two parameters of the plane by accounting for the distortions that arise when a nonplanar spherical surface is transferred to a planar surface. This mechanism underlies the creation of maps that are a planar model of the nonplanar surface of the Earth.

Flat coordinate systems. The choice of the coordinate system depends on the size of the surface areas to be studied and, consequently, on the influence of the Earth's curvature. When depicting small areas of the Earth, a part of the level surface can be taken as a plane. Such areas will be plots up to 20 km long and up to 400 km square^2 . In these cases plane coordinates are applicable Fig.4.1. They can be either Cartesian or polar.

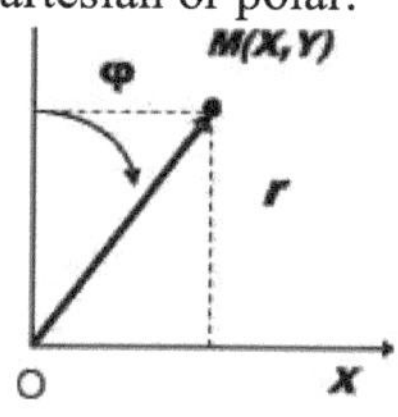

Figure 4.1. Plane Cartesian and polar coordinates

Plane Cartesian coordinates are defined by specifying two axes. In this case usually X coordinate points to the east, Y - to the north. The angle f (Fig.4.1) is called the directional angle. Scale segments are set to connect coordinates of systems with real sizes of objects. The ordered pair (X, Y) will determine the position of a point in the given system. The point of intersection is called the coordinate axes the origin or zero of the coordinate system. The abscissa axis is OX and the ordinate axis is OY.

There are two systems of rectangular coordinates: left and right. In geodesy, the left system is more commonly used. The position of a point in the rectangular system is uniquely defined by two coordinates X and Y; X coordinate expresses the distance of the point from the OY axis, Y coordinate

- the distance from the OY axis. The coordinate values are positive (with "+" sign) and negative (with "-" sign) depending on the quarter in which the point is located.

Planar polar coordinates use the distance from the origin (*r*) and the angle (φ) from a fixed direction. The direction is usually fixed to north, and the angle is counted clockwise from it. Polar coordinates are convenient when taking measurements from a given point. If it is necessary to take into account the curvature of the Earth, spatial coordinate systems are used.

4.3. Earth coordinate systems

Terrestrial coordinate systems have differences from ideal mathematical coordinate systems because they are related to the shape of the Earth object, which is not strictly described by a simple mathematical figure. Terrestrial coordinate systems were developed by two directions: geodetic and astronomical.

Historically, determining the position of an object on the Earth's surface was related to astronomical observations of the starry sky. The geodetic approach is concerned with studying the shape of the Earth and relating objects on its surface into a unified system. It uses models of the Earth's surface to determine latitude and longitude. It follows that latitude in the geodetic approach is related to the shape of the Earth's surface. The theory of the Earth's shape has evolved and, as a consequence, the coordinate systems associated with it have evolved.

The astronomical approach is related to the determination of the position of the object on the Earth's surface by the starry sky. In this case there was no doubt about the spherical construction of the celestial sphere. Hence arose spherical geometry, which has its roots in Arabic science and has defined a number of terms up to the present time. When analysing the terminology, it should be noted that in European scientific language, particularly in the theory of coordinate systems, there are many Arabic words, such as algebra, almucantarat, azimuth, zenith, nadir and others.

Almucantarat (Arabic) [4] the arc of a small circle formed by the section of the celestial sphere, by a plane parallel to the plane of the horizon. All points of the almukantarat have equal astronomical heights above the horizon.

This concept, transferred to cartography, is used to denote a special family of lines on the surface of the globe (Earth model). Such a line is a geometric place of points equidistant from any selected point on the surface of the globe. If such chosen point is a geographical pole of the Earth then almucantarata will be geographical parallels. Almucantarata are a stable element of coordinate systems. On geographical maps they can be represented by different types of curves or straight lines depending on the way of map projection.

Vertical (from Latin *verticalis* - plumb) [4] as well as almucantarat has two meanings astronomical and cartographic. In astronomy, a vertical is a large circle of the celestial sphere passing through the zenith and nadir. The vertical perpendicular to the celestial meridian is called the *first vertical,* and the points of its intersection with the celestial horizon are called the west and east points. In cartography, a vertical is a family of lines on the surface of the globe (Earth model) complementing the almucantarata as elements of the coordinate system. Verticals are each large circle passing through the pole of spherical coordinates.

The vertical passing through the geographical pole coincides with the meridian. The position of verticals on the cartographic surface is determined by azimuth " *a* ", which is equal to dihedral angle between the planes of the current and initial verticals. The initial vertical is the vertical that coincides with the meridian of the pole of the oblique or transverse coordinate systems.

Almucantarats are arcs of small circles orthogonal to verticals; their position on the mapped surface is determined by the zenith distance *z*, equal to the arc of the vertical from the pole of the adopted coordinate system to the current almucantarat.

Zenith is the point of the sky lying at the top [4]. A distinction is made between geographic and geocentric zeniths. *Geographic zenith* is defined as a point in the direction of the plumb line, in every place of the Earth's surface. *Geocentric zenith* is defined as a point lying above, in the direction of the continuation of the line connecting the place of observation with the centre of the Earth.

If the Earth were a sphere, both zeniths would coincide. However, due to the difference in the shape of the Earth from the spherical shape, the geocentric zenith differs from the geographic zenith between the equator and the pole. Their angular distance is insignificant and reaches its greatest value (about 12') at latitudes of about ±45°.

The angular distance of any luminary from the zenith is called the zenith distance. Depending on whether the distance is considered from the geographic or geocentric zenith, geographic and geocentric zenith distances are distinguished. The addition of the zenith distance to 90° is called the altitude of the luminary.

Nadir is a point opposite to the zenith, lying downwards, in the direction of the plumb line, at every place on the earth's surface. Such a point is invisible directly and is obtained artificially by placing a vessel of mercury or a horizontal mirror under the instrument: the nadir can be regarded as an image of the zenith on the earth's surface.

In practice, astronomical and geodetic coordinates are widely used. The following elements are used in these coordinate systems [4]:

Earth's equatorial plane - a plane that passes through the centre of the Earth perpendicular to its axis of rotation;

plane of the geographical (astronomical) *meridian* - passes through the Earth's axis of rotation and a plumb line at a point on the Earth's surface;

meridian - the line of intersection of the planes of geographical meridians with the Earth surface;

parallel - a line formed by the intersection of a plane parallel to the plane of the Earth's equator with the Earth's surface.

The position of a point in the astronomical (geographic) coordinate system is determined by latitude (f) and longitude (a) (Fig.4.1). The position of the point in the geodetic coordinate system is determined by latitude (*B*) and longitude (*L*).

Latitude (geodetic) - the angle between the normal to the surface of the ellipsoid and the equatorial plane. It varies from -90° (south pole) to +90° (north pole).

Latitude (astronomical) - the angle between the plumb line at a given point on the surface and the plane of the equator.

Longitude is the angle in the plane of the equator between the meridian of a point and the prime (zero) meridian passing through Greenwich, England. It varies from -180° (west longitude) to +180° (east longitude).

The basic concepts of these coordinate systems are: *meridian* - line of constant longitude; *parallel* - line of constant latitude;

great circle - an imaginary circle on the Earth's surface formed by a plane passing through the centre of the globe;

small circle - an imaginary circle on the Earth's surface formed by a plane not passing through the centre of the globe.

Coordinate surfaces in these systems are the surface of a sphere or ellipsoid, level surfaces, secant planes parallel to the equator, secant planes passing through the Earth's axis.

The coordinate lines in these systems are.

$B = const\ (\varphi = const)$ family of parallels (almucantharata).

$L = const\ (\lambda = const)$ meridian family.

The peculiarity of the choice of such coordinate lines is dictated by the need to transfer information from the surface of the Earth model to the flat surface of the map. These coordinate lines define the geographic grid, which is displayed

in the selected projection.
Coordinate systems used in geodesy and geoinformatics are chosen depending on the tasks to be solved. Different mathematical surface models and different coordinate systems are used to represent the position of surface points on the plane. In practice, planar and spherical ones are used more often. Less often curvilinear or polar ones are used. If we choose the type of coordinate lines as an aspect of classification, we obtain the following classification of coordinate systems:
rectangular coordinates *(X, Y)* - in the plane;
rectangular coordinates *(X, Y, Z)-in* space, curvilinear coordinates: spherical - on a sphere, ellipsoidal - on an ellipsoid, the latter are often called geodesic coordinates.

4.4. Varieties of terrestrial coordinate systems.

There are geodetic, astronomical and geographic coordinate systems (Fig. 4.2) [4]. All three systems use the concept of latitude and longitude. As already mentioned, the geodetic coordinate system is related to the figure of the Earth and the correlation of objects on its surface into a single system. It uses models of the Earth's surface to determine latitude and longitude. It follows that latitude in this approach is related to the shape of the Earth's surface. Since an ellipsoid with variable surface curvature is chosen as the model, the latitude on such a surface will be different from the latitude determined for a model with constant curvature in the form of a spheroid.
The astronomical approach is associated with determining the position of an object on the Earth's surface using a starry sky or sphere model. The latter has a constant curvature. Hence the difference in the definition of astronomical latitude as the angle between the centre of the sphere or the direction of the plumb line to the centre of the Earth without regard to the curvature of the surface. An important conclusion astronomical and geodetic latitude in some points of the Earth's surface though insignificantly, but differ.
What are geographical coordinates? There is no unambiguous answer in the domestic literature. The first approach [4], is that geographic coordinates are a generalised concept of geodetic and astronomical coordinates. The second approach [4] is that geographic coordinates are the same as astronomical coordinates.

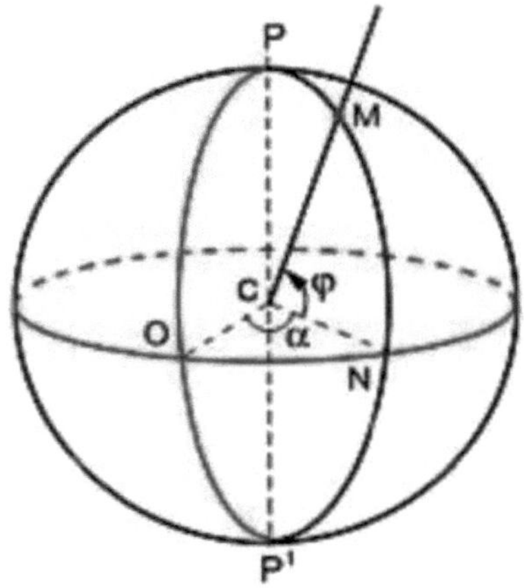

Figure 4.6. Geographical coordinates

Fig.4.6 shows the geographic coordinates. Line RR' The axis of rotation. Point M- point on the Earth's surface. C- the centre of mass of the Earth. O- zero meridian. In relation to the Earth, geocentric, reference and topocentric coordinate systems are distinguished.

Geocentric coordinate systems are associated with the centre of the Earth. They are closer to astronomical ones. These coordinate systems are based on the *model of the all-Earth ellipsoid*, namely the ellipsoid of rotation, plane of the equator and the centre of which coincides with the equatorial plane and the centre of mass of the Earth and best approximates the surface of a geoid (quasigeoid).

Reference coordinate systems are associated with the figure of the *reference ellipsoid.* These systems are used for the territory of a particular country or several countries. As a rule, reference ellipsoids *are legally* accepted for processing geodetic measurements. Orientation of the reference ellipsoid in the Earth's body is subject to the following requirements:

1. The differences between astronomical and geodetic coordinates should be minimal
2. The minor semi-major axis of the ellipsoid (b) must be parallel to the Earth's axis of rotation.
3. The surface of the ellipsoid should be as close as possible to the surface of the geoid within a given region (for countries with a large area) or for a country (for countries with a small area).

Unlike the all-Earth ellipsoid, to orientate and anchor the reference ellipsoid in the Earth's body it is necessary to set initial geodetic dates (*datum*).

4.5. Geocentric and topocentric coordinate systems

Geocentric coordinate systems are used primarily for navigation when moving objects in near-Earth space, when the shape of the Earth (or another planet) does not play an essential role. The theory of geocentric (planetocentric) coordinate systems can be used to create coordinate systems for any objects of the Solar System or objects of other galaxies.

In practice, different coordinate systems are used: geocentric, topocentric, polar geodetic, ecliptic, etc. If we choose coordinate origins as an aspect of analysis, we can talk about geocentric, quasigeocentric and topocentric - coordinate systems (Fig.4.7). Thus, the geocentric system is related to the concept of the Earth model as a *universal ellipsoid.* Different realisations of this model are used

GRS80 (Geodetic Reference System 1980) was developed by the International Union of Geodesy and Geophysics and is recommended for geodetic work;

WGS84 (World Geodetic System 1984) is used in the GPS satellite navigation system;

P390 (Earth Parameters 1990) is used on the territory of Russia for geodetic support of orbital flights. This ellipsoid is used in the GLONASS satellite navigation system;

IERS96 (International Earth Rotation Service 1996) is recommended by the International Earth Rotation Service for processing VLBI observations

The *geocentric* coordinate system *(X, Y, Z)* is a system of coordinates *(X, Y, Z)* with the origin *O* coinciding with the centre of mass of the Earth (Fig. 4.7).

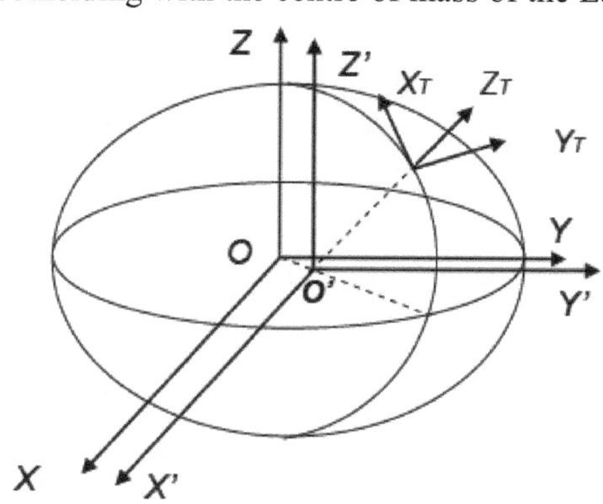

Fig.4.7 Geocentric, quasi-geocentric and topocentric coordinate systems

If the origin of the system O' is located near the centre of mass of the Earth (within a few hundred metres), then such a coordinate system *(X', Y', Z')* is called *quasigeocentric.*

The Z axis points to the Earth's north pole. The *X* axis is directed to the point of intersection of the equator with the Greenwich meridian. *The Y* axis completes the formed equatorial system to the right.
Topocentric (from Greek *topos* - place) coordinate system is a coordinate system (Fig. 4.7), in which direct geodetic measurements and works on the Earth's surface are performed. As a rule, it is a Cartesian coordinate system associated with reference.
Topocentric coordinate system is a coordinate system (X_T, Y_T, Z_T) with the origin at or near the Earth's surface. *THE* Z_T axis coincides with the normal to the surface of the Earth's ellipsoid. The *Xt* axis lies in the meridian plane and is directed to the north pole. *THE* Y_T axis completes the formed system to the left. The system participates in the daily rotation of the Earth, remaining stationary relative to the points of the Earth's surface and therefore is convenient for navigation and determination of the position of objects relative to the Earth's surface.

4.6. Geodetic coordinates

Geodetic coordinates are also defined by the latitude and longitude of points on the Earth's surface. However, their determination is made with the help of geodetic measurements. When analysing these coordinate systems use geocentric (spheroidal) F, reduced *U* and geodetic *B* - latitudes shown in Fig. 4.8.
Figure 4.8 shows a fragment of a section of an ellipsoid of rotation by a meridian plane. The canonical equation of the ellipse obtained as a result of such a section has the form

$$\frac{x^2}{a^2} + \frac{z^2}{b^2} = 1 \quad (4.1)$$

There is a point T on the ellipse which has different values of geodetic, reduced and geocentric latitude.
The advantage of the spheroidal system is that the spheroid has a surface of equal curvature, as a consequence of which calculations in the transition from curvilinear coordinates to Cartesian coordinates are considerably simplified.
For a circle and a sphere, the equation of the normal to the surface is a straight line passing through the centre of the circle or sphere. The point T (Fig. 4.8) has in this system a latitude value equal to F. An ellipsoid has a surface of variable curvature. For its section, the normal equation for the point T will pass away from the centre of symmetry and will be characterised by the geodesic latitude *B*.

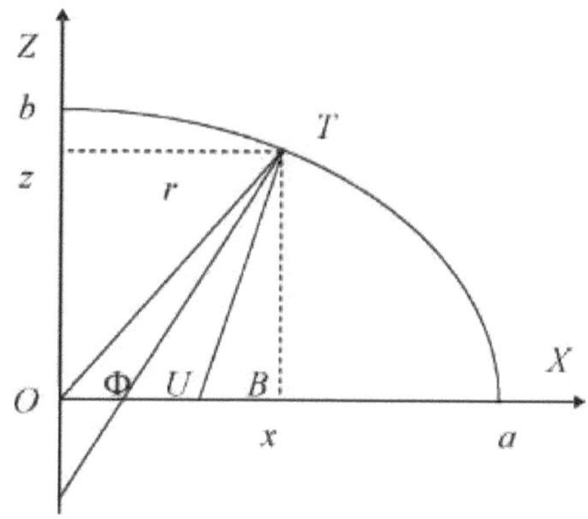

Fig.4.8. Geocentric, reduced and geodetic latitudes

The ellipse in Fig. 4.8 has major semi-axis a and minor semi-axis b. The radius of the almucantarate (parallel) for the point T is r. It coincides with the Cartesian coordinate of this point in the *ZOX* system. Let's use the angle of the reduced latitude U for the point T. It is constructed on the basis of notching of the axis OZ from the point T with the radius equal to the major semi-major axis a. This makes it possible to construct the relation

$$r=x=a \cos U \quad (4.2)$$

Using the expression (4.1.) we obtain the value for the *z-coordinate* of the point T.

$$z= b \sin U \quad (4.3)$$

It is possible to define the reduced latitude as the direction associated with the circles of small and large radii of the ellipsoid section (Fig.4.9). Small and large radii are equal respectively to the small and large semi-axes of the ellipse obtained as a section of the ellipsoid. The centre of the circle of small radius moves along the X axis. The centre of the circle of large radius moves along the Z axis (Fig.4.8). The circles have a common point A on the surface of the ellipsoid where they touch. As point A moves along the surface of the ellipsoid, the centre of the large circle slides along the Z axis, the centre of the small circle along the X axis, so that their points of touch always coincide.

Thus, the given latitude is the angle between the *X-axis* and the radius of a large circle to point A, sliding along the *Z-axis*, so that the radius of the small circle sliding along the *X-axis*, touching point A, coincides with the radius of the large circle. Both circles have point A as a common point of tangency. The spatial coordinates of the point on the surface of the ellipsoid are defined by

$$X= N \cos B \cos L; \; Y= N \cos B \sin L; \; Z=N (1- e^2) \sin B \quad (4.4).$$

Here *N is the* radius of the first vertical passing through the point T on the surface of the ellipsoid [4].

4.7. Reference coordinate systems

Reference coordinate systems [4] are used to determine the coordinates of points within a country or region. *The reference ellipsoid* is an earth ellipsoid, which is the best approximation of the geoid surface within the area provided by the coordinate system. When determining the parameters of the reference ellipsoid, the task of aligning the centres of the ellipsoid and the Earth is usually not set. In Russia, the reference ellipsoid is the Krasovsky ellipsoid and its associated 1942 coordinate system (SK-42). According to the Decree of the Council of Ministers of the Russian Federation No. 568 of 2000, since 1 July 2002 the transition to the new reference coordinate system SK-95 has been carried out. In SK-95 the dimensions of the Krasovsky ellipsoid (a=6378245 m, a=0,003352329869) and the former coordinates of the Pulkovo Astronomical Observatory are preserved, and the coordinate axes are directed parallel to the coordinate axes of PZ-90.

Coordinates of the state geodetic network are expressed in the reference system, maps are compiled and published. At the same time, spatial coordinates are preferred to more visible geodetic coordinates (latitude, longitude and altitude).

From the late seventeenth century to the second half of the nineteenth century, a figure close to an ellipsoid of rotation was used as the shape of the Earth. From the second half of the nineteenth century to the 1940s, a triaxial ellipsoid was used as a model of the Earth. The triaxial ellipsoid is only an approximation of the more complex geoid shape. A geoid is defined using the concept of a level surface.

A level surface is a surface, each point of which is orthogonal to the gravity vector of a given celestial body.

A set of level surfaces defines *a height system.* In each country the initial level surface has its initial height point, so altitude systems differ from country to country. In Russia, the Baltic altitude system is accepted.

The Baltic height system is a system for which the initial level surface passes through the zero point of the Kronstatt Footstock.

The surface of a geoid is the level surface passing through the origin of the elevation.

The strict definition of geoid is related to the knowledge of the structure of the Earth's crust. It should be noted that there are so-called gravitational anomalies on the Earth, due to which the level surface cannot be a convenient mathematical model. Therefore, in practice, the concept of quasigeoid is used.

This figure can be defined without hypotheses about the structure of the Earth's crust, it has a smoother (regular) surface compared to the geoid. *The surface of the quasigeoid* coincides with the surface of the geoid on the seas and oceans and recedes from it up to 2 metres on the continental part of the Earth. It should be recalled that the centres of masses of the land and the world ocean do not coincide.

The Earth's surface has a complex shape. Of its total surface area of 510 million kilometres^2 , 71% is the bottom of the seas and oceans and 29% is land. This gives reason to believe that the Earth's surface consists of two sharply different morphological elements - continents and oceans.

The *all-Earth ellipsoid* is an ellipsoid of rotation whose equatorial plane and centre coincide with the equatorial plane and centre of mass of the Earth and best approximates the surface of a geoid (quasigeoid).

Reference ellipsoid is an ellipsoid of rotation, on the surface of which the materials of astronomical-geodetic works, topographic surveys and geodetic are mapped.

The ellipsoid obtained by F. Bessel was used in the USSR until 1946. Its parameters:

The major semi-major axis a is 6377397.155 metres.

The minor semi-major axis b is 6356079 m.

Compression (a-b)/f is 1:299.1528128.

In 1946, the ellipsoid calculated in the Central Research Institute of Geophysics and Geophysics in 1940 under the direction of F.N. Krasovsky with the participation of A.A. Izotov was introduced for mandatory use in the USSR. Its parameters: Major semi-major axis a - 6378245 m. Small semi-major axis b - 6356863.0188 m. Compression (a-b)/f - 1:298.3

Overseas, especially in foreign GIS software, the Clark ellipsoid is widely used as a reference. There are two kinds of Clark I and Clark II. Their parameters are given in Table 4.1

Table 4.1. Parameters of the Clark ellipsoid [300].

	Clark I	Clarke II
Major axis a	6378206 м	6378249 м
Minor semi-major axis b	6356584 м	6356515 м
Compression (a- b)/f	1:294.9786982	1:293.465

CHAPTER 5

5. Analyses in applied geoinformatics

5.1. Geoinformation approach

There is a concept of information approach. Geoinformatics has its own approach - geoinformation approach. It is reasonable to compare geoinformation and information approaches. Both approaches include the use of: information units [301-305], models, monitoring, modelling, information flows.

Geoinformation approach includes the use of: spatial models, digital models, digital maps, geoinformation models, geoinformation monitoring, geoinformation modelling. Structurally, the geoinformation approach to the analysis of processes and phenomena is shown in Fig. 5.1. Let us consider its features [234].

Fig.5.1 Geoinformation approach

The allocation of three groups of data "place" "time" "topic" allows for the classification of different data and their subsequent integration into a unified information framework. The first three steps are not applied in informatics.

Digital models and digital maps have an integrating function, which makes it possible to combine heterogeneous information resources. The integrating function makes it possible to create a hypertext structure of the data included in the information base

Graphical and cartographic visual models in geoinformatics represent a vast information space. This space includes many relationships between real-world objects and their attributes. Data stratification with the inclusion of hierarchy relations means the creation of a hierarchical model, visually represented as a set of layers with common themes and attributes. The fundamental thing in such a description is the possibility of using logical and set-theoretic operations to obtain new knowledge about the objects of exploration and phenomena on the Earth's surface.

Identifying spatial relationships makes it possible to find weak and strong, explicit and implicit connections between objects located at different points in space.

Visual modelling is key in the representation, interpretation and processing of geodata. The volume and complexity of geodata is so large that traditional methods of analysing (simple) information become unacceptable. Let us analyse the differences between the information approach and the geoinformation approach.

The information approach is aimed at processing any information and solving any problems, but requires adaptation of processing technologies to the data of the subject area (types, scale, accuracy). Geoinformation approach is aimed at processing integrated spatial information, geodata and solving problems related to the positioning and movement of objects on the Earth's surface. It is aimed at solving problems related to the occurrence, course and disappearance of various processes and phenomena on the Earth's surface. It does not require adaptation of technologies as it uses integrated geodata.

The information approach plays the role of an intermediary in processing the initial data collected by the user and solving the tasks set by the user. Geo-information approach plays the role of integrator in solving the user's tasks. The information approach is more processing-oriented, without regard to applications. This determines its instrumental character and allows it to be used with the involvement of an intermediary - a programmer.

Geoinformation approach is focused not only on processing, but also on generalisation and analysis of information with the target output - obtaining management information or information for decision support. This determines its integrative character and allows to consider it as a tool of a subject matter expert, for example, in cartography and medicine.

The information approach appeared earlier and was oriented on data processing without regard to spatial relations. Historically, the geoinformational approach appeared later, but it takes into account the shortcomings of the informational approach and adds specificity, allowing to find and use spatial relations to solve a set of problems. The coordinate environment factor is absent in the information approach. The factor of coordinate environment in the geoinformation approach is present and plays

an integrating key role.
The information approach aims at identifying and modelling relationships. The geo-information approach aims at identifying and utilising linkages and relationships, among which spatial relationships play a leading role.
The information approach is characterised by an intermediary aspect between processing methods and applications. The geo-information approach is characterised by an integrative aspect.
Thus, the geoinformation approach has its own specificity and certain advantages in relation to the tasks related to spatial relations and spatial distribution of any information (economic, historical, biological). It should be stated that geoinformatics and informatics have their own research methods and their own fields of application.

5.2. Categorical analysis in applied geoinformatics

In geoinformatics, all fixed parameters are represented using quantitative and qualitative characteristics. Categories, measurement scales and variables defined in these measurement scales are used to distinguish and compare measurements. Category is a more general concept in relation to quality.
There is a theory of categories [306], which studies the properties of relations between objects that do not depend on the internal structure of objects. In mathematics these are mathematical objects in geoinformatics these are spatial objects, in informatics these are information objects
Category theory occupies an important place in modern mathematics; it has found applications in computer science [307], in logic [308] and in theoretical physics and geoinformatics. The modern exposition of algebraic geometry and homological algebra relies heavily on the concepts of category theory. General concepts of categories are also actively used in the language of functional programming [306].
Category theory formalises mathematical structure and its concepts using a labelled directed graph called a category. The nodes of such a graph are called objects, and labelled directed edges are called arrows (or morphisms). [306]
As defined by Eilenberg & Mac Lane [309] "A Category (C) is a set of Ob abstract elements called Category C *objects* and Map abstract elements called category *mappings*
The category has two main properties. The ability to form arrows associatively. The existence of an arrow identity for each object. The language of category theory has been used to formalise the concepts of other high-level abstractions such as sets, rings and groups. Informally, category theory is a general theory of functions. Some terms used in category theory, including the term "morphism", are interpreted differently from the rest of mathematics. In

category theory, morphisms are subject to conditions specific to category theory itself.

Categories are generalisations or abstractions of many concepts: mathematical, physical, logical, spatial, analytical, geoinformatics. Many fields of sciences can be formalised by category theory as categories, including geoinformatics. Category theory based on generalisation makes it possible to formulate and prove many complex mathematical and empirical results in a simple formal way.

An example of categories is the category of sets, in which objects are sets and arrows are functions of transformations from one set to another. The objects of the category do not have to be sets, and the arrows do not have to be functions. They can show relations. Any way of formalising the theory so that it satisfies the basic conditions for the behaviour of objects and arrows is a valid category, and all the results of category theory apply to it. This is what makes it possible to use category theory in geoinformatics.

Morphisms or "arrows" in category theory represent a process (relation, transformation) connecting two objects. In many cases, a morphism preserves the structure of the objects it connects. There are many applications in which concepts are represented by objects and morphisms. The most important property of morphisms is that they can be "composed", that is, arranged in such a sequence that creates a new morphism.

The application of categories is an axiomatic approach to describe various classes of related mathematical or spatial structures associated with transformation functions while preserving the structure between them. The application of category theory allows us to prove general results about any of the types of analytic structures based on the original categorical axioms.

For example, group homomorphism between two groups "preserves group structure" in the precise sense. Empirically, it is a process of transition from one group to another in which information about the structure of the first group is transferred to the second group. The study of group homomorphisms then provides a tool for studying general properties of groups and implications of group axioms. Category C - consists of the following three formal objects

1. class of objects Ob_C or Ob(C), whose elements are called objects
2. class Hom_C (A, B) or Hom (C), or f - whose elements are called morphisms or arrows. Each morphism f has a source object A and a target object B (Fig. 5.2).

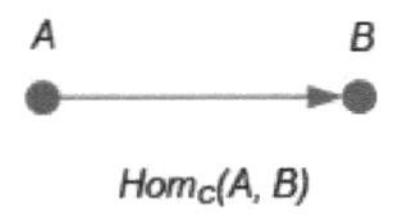

Figure 5.2. Morphism

In Fig. 5.2, A is a category object, B is a category mapping, and the arrow is a morphism. Thus each morphism corresponds to the only A and B. The expression $f: A \to B$ means "f is a morphism from *A* to *B*". The expression Hom$_C$
(A, B) - alternatively expressed as mor *(A, B)* or C *(A, B)* - denotes the *hom-class of* all morphisms from *A* to *B*.

3. A binary operation or morphism composition such that for a pair of morphisms $f: A \to B$ *and* $g: B \to C$, the composition $g \bullet f (A \to C)$ is defined (Figure5.3);

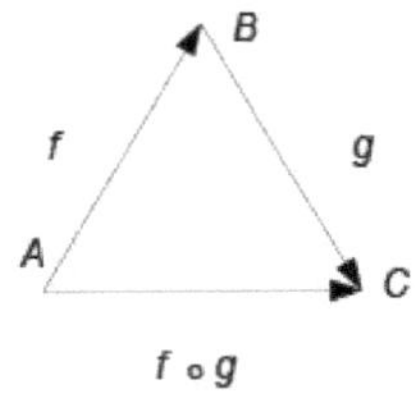

Figure 5.3. Composition of morphisms

Composition obeys two axioms

Associativity if $f: a \to b$, $g: b \to c$ and $h: c \to d$, to
$h \circ (g \circ f) = (h \circ g) \circ f$

Identity. For each object A there is an identity morphism id$_a$ $a \to a$, , such that for any morphism $f: a \to b$, , we have $id_b \circ f = f = f \circ id_a$

From the axioms we can prove that for every object there is exactly one identity morphism or identity morphism.

Figure 1.2.1 can be interpreted in many different ways. Examples.

A - object parameters, B - results of parameters measurement, Hom$_C$ (A, B) - process of parameters measurement.

A - image, B - image scan, Home (A, B) - image scanning process.

A - original photo, B - transformed photo, Hom$_C$
(A, B) - the process of transforming the image.

A - primary measurements, B - unified measurements, Hom$_C$ (A, B) - process of unification of primary measurements.

Minor category. A class of objects is not necessarily a set in the sense of axiomatic set theory. A category C in which Ob_C is a set and Hom (C) (the set of all morphisms of the category) is a set is called a small category. It is also possible (with a slight correction of the definition) to consider categories in which the morphisms between any two objects also form a class, or even a larger structure [306]. In this variant of the definition, a category in which morphisms between two fixed objects form a set is called locally small.

Examples of categories

Set is a category of sets. Objects in this category are sets, morphisms are mappings of sets.

Data - data category. Objects in this category are data, morphisms are data mappings or data transformations.

Geodata - geodata category. Objects in this category are data, morphisms are geodata mappings

Model - category of models. Objects in this category are models, morphisms are mappings of models, transformation of models into new models

Information model - category of information models. Objects in this category are information models, morphisms are information transformations, information interactions, information relations.

Spatial information situation - category of spatial information situations. Objects in this category are information situations, morphisms are spatial situational transformations, spatial relations

Spatial 3D model - a category of spatial 3D models. Objects in this category are three-dimensional spatial models, morphisms are spatial transformations (in particular, forward and backward serifs).

Spatial 2D model - category of spatial flat models. Objects in this category are plane models and plane images, morphisms are spatial transformations (transforming, scanning, image enhancement, image processing).

Geoinformation model is a category of geoinformation models. Objects in this category are geoinformation models, morphisms are geoinformation transformations and geoinformation modelling.

Digital model - category of digital models. Objects in this category are digital models, morphisms are digital transformations.

Grp is a category of groups. Objects are groups, morphisms are mappings preserving the group structure (homomorphisms of groups).

VectK is a category of vector spaces over a field K. Morphisms are linear mappings.

Top - category of topological spaces. Morphisms - continuous (conformal) mappings (e.g. transformations of cartographic projections).

A partially ordered set is a category whose objects are elements of a set, and there is a single morphism between elements x and y if and only if $x<y$. Morphisms are qualitative and quantitative relations.

Met is a category whose objects are metric spaces and whose morphisms are short mappings.

Categories for other systems are defined in the same way.

Commutative diagrams. The standard way of describing relations in category theory is commutative diagrams (Fig. 5.4). A commutative diagram is an oriented graph whose vertices contain category objects and whose arrows are morphisms, and the result of the composition of arrows does not depend on the chosen path. For example, the axioms of category theory (associativity of composition and the property of identity morphism) can be written with the help of diagrams

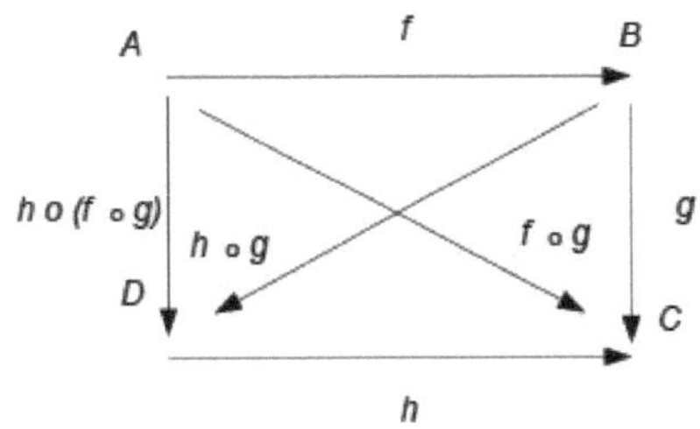

Fig. 5.4 Commutative diagram

Morphisms can have any of the following properties.

monomorphism (or monic), if $f \circ g_1 = f \circ g_2$ then this entails $gi = g2$ for all morphisms $g_1, g_2\colon x \to a$.

epimorphism (or epic), if $g_1 \circ f = g_2 \circ f$ then this entails $g1 = g_2$ for all morphisms $g_1, g_2\colon b \to x$.

bimorphism if *f is* both epic and monic.

isomorphism if there exists a morphism $g\colon b \to a$ such that $f \circ g = id_b$ and $g \circ f = id_a$. [b]

endomorphism, if a = b, then end(a) denotes the class of endomorphisms of a

.

automorphism, if *f* is both an endomorphism and an isomorphism, then aut (a) denotes the class of automorphisms of a.

retraction if the right inverse *f* exists, i.e. if there exists a morphism $g\colon b \to a$ c $f \circ g = id_b$

section (section) if the left inverse of *f* exists, i.e., if there exists a morphism $g\colon b \to a$ c $g \circ f = id_a$

Duality. For category C, we can define a dual category C^{op} , in which: objects coincide with the objects of the original category; morphisms are obtained by "arrow reversal": Hom cop (B, A) "Home (A, B)

The principle of duality states that for any statement of the theory of categories it is possible to formulate a dual statement by means of arrow reversal and the truth of the statement will not change. Often a dual concept is denoted by the same term with the prefix "co", for example: sine - cosine; tangent - cotangent, covariant vector - contravariant vector. For example, a contravariant vector is a column vector, a covariant vector is a row vector.

Initial and terminal objects. An initial (initial, universally repulsive) object of a category is such an object from which a single morphism exists into any object of the category. If initial objects in a category exist, they are all isomorphic. A doubly defined terminal or universally attracting object is one into which a single morphism exists from any object in the category. A category object is called null if it is both initial and terminal.

Example: In the Set category, the initial object is the empty set $\varnothing$, , the terminal object is any set of one element {.}.

Example: There is a null object in the Grp category, which is a group of one item.

The product and the sum of objects. The product of objects can change the category, while the sum preserves it. The product of a pair of objects A and B is an object (A x B) with morphisms $p_1: A \times B \to A$ and $p_2: A \times B \to B$, , such that for any object C with morphisms $f_1: C \to A$ and $f_2: C \to B$ there exists a single morphism $h: C \to A \times B$, , such that the diagram in Fig5.5 is commutative.

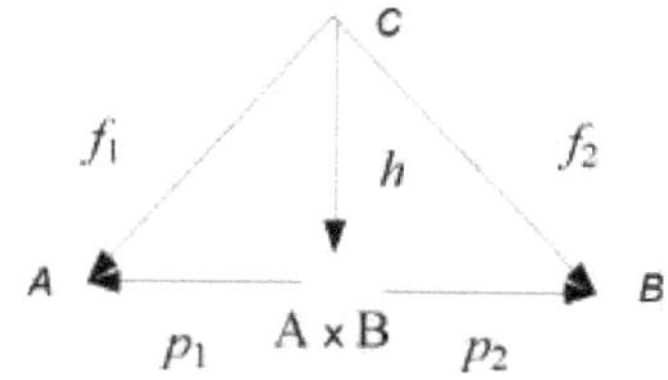

Figure 5.5. Derivation of categorical objects

Morphisms $p_1: A \times B \to A$ и $p_2: A \times B \to B$ are called projections.

Example: In the category Set, the product of A and B is a direct product in the sense of set theory A x B.

In the Data category, the product of X, Y, Z is the direct product or the Cartesian coordinate system X x Y x Z.

Morphisms p_1: X × Y × Z →X , p_2: X × Y × Z →Y, p_3: X × Y × Z →Z are called projections. A morphism in the Cartesian coordinate system is a projection of a spatial object into a plane (not necessarily a coordinate plane). Morphisms - projections change the category (Fig. 5.6).

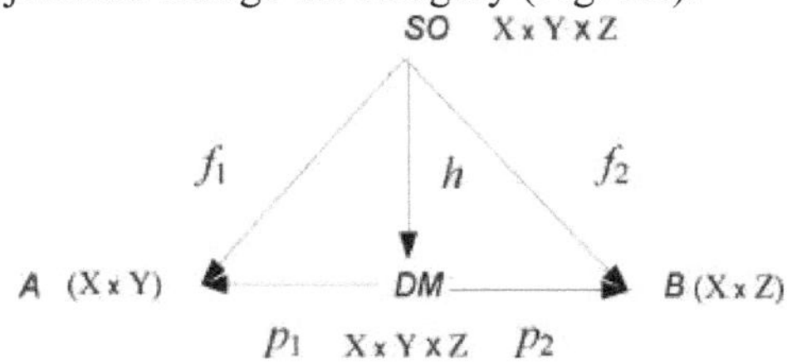

Fig5.6. Categories of spatial transformations

In Fig5.6, SO(X x Y x Z) is a spatial 3D object, morphism f_1: SO →A - is aerial photography, morphism f_2: SO →B - is ground-based photography, and morphism h: SO →DM - is the construction of a spatial digital model. Ground photography f_2 or aerial photography *f1* changes the category. Mobile laser scanning *h* retains the category.

Functors (Fig. 5.7) are functions that preserve the structure between categories. They can be considered as morphisms in the categories of all (small) categories.

The covariate functor *F* from category *C* to category *D*, denoted by *F*: *C* *D*, includes the properties:

for each object *x* in *C, an* object *F (x)* in *D*; and

for each morphism $f: x \rightarrow y$ in *C* morphism $F(f): F(x) \rightarrow F(y)$, ,

such that the following two properties hold

For each object *x* in C, $F(Id_x) = Id_{F(x)}$;

For all morphisms $f: x \rightarrow y$ и $g: y \rightarrow z$, $F(g \circ f) = F(g) \circ F(f)$.

The contravariant functor$F: C \rightarrow D$ behaves like a covariant functor, except that it inverts all arrows. More specifically, every morphism $F: x \rightarrow y$ in *C* must be assigned a morphism $F(f): F(y) \rightarrow F(x)$ в *D*. . In other words, the contravariant functor

acts as a covariate functor from the oppositional category *C* to *D*.

If *F* and *G* are (covariant) functors between categories *C* and *D*, then the natural transformation η from *F* to *G* maps to every object X in C a morphism $\eta X: F(X) \rightarrow G(X)$ in D such that for any morphism $f: X \rightarrow Y$ in C we have $\eta Y \circ F(f) = G(X) \circ \eta X$; this means that the following diagram is commutative

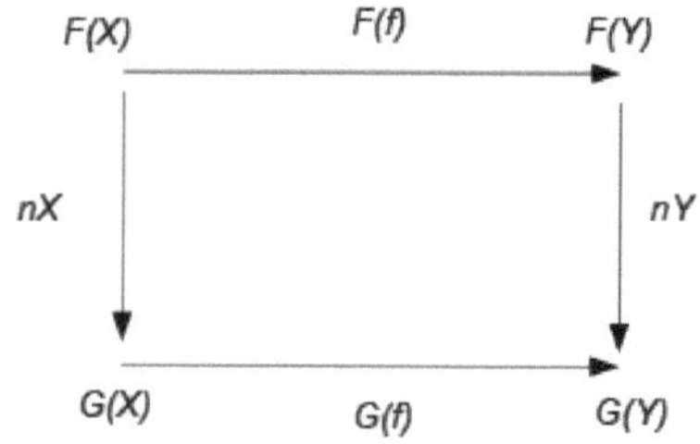

Figure 5.7. Functors

Two functors *F* and *G* are called *naturally isomorphic* if there exists a natural transformation from *F* to *G* such that nX is an isomorphism for every object *X* in *C*.

Category theory gives geoinformatics a formalism for the generalised study of processes and phenomena in theory writing and knowledge transfer.

5.3. Complexity in geoinformatics

The problem of complexity exists in applied geoinformatics as well as in many scientific fields. There are many models of Complexity from combinatorics models [310] to graph-based crisp and fuzzy complexity models [311]. Complexity in geoinformatics is due to technological complexity, modelling complexity and computational complexity. These types of complexity include structural complexity and topological complexity.

Complexity in geoinformatics is due to the possible risk of decision making [312]. Complexity in geoinformatics is due to the complexity of algorithms that are used in information processing [313]. As one of the tools to reduce algorithmic complexity I use conceptual programming [314].

Geoinformation technologies is a broad concept that includes work with GIS and other technologies, such as satellite navigation technologies, construction of spatial models on the basis of mobile laser scanning, CAD application technologies, mathematical spatial modelling, solving problems of geodetic and photogrammetric constructions, application of spatial logic and other types of work. In the processes of application of geoinformation technologies the concept of "complexity" arises. Complexity as a characteristic of computational processes is well researched in the field of computing and in this field there is a term "computational complexity". Complexity as a characteristic of a system is used in system analysis, where it is close to the notion of structural complexity. In psychology, cognitive science and education there is the concept of cognitive complexity [315]. In comparative analysis there is the concept of comparative complexity. In design, there is the concept of construction complexity and decomposition complexity. In cartography, there is the notion of topological complexity of maps [316]. In software exploitation systems, in integrated information systems, the concept of accumulated quality [317] is applied, which reduces the complexity of exploitation. To analyse complexity in geoinformatics, we should consider generalised geoinformation processing.

A generalised geoinformation processing scheme.

Geo-information processing includes the stages of description collection, modelling and computer processing. The system of geoinformation information processing is a technological system with separate parts. The basis of research and processing is the object of reality, which is understood as: spatial object, phenomenon, spatial process or spatial regularity. Spatial regularity is often expressed through spatial relations. A primary description or infological model is formed for the object of research. This model contains the results of data collection, which is carried out using different technologies. The infological model is a partially formalised model, which requires refinement at subsequent stages of research.

To transform an infological model [318] into a geoinformation model, it should be decomposed into parts that can be conveniently modelled and processed. Such decomposition requires sets of information units and stereotypes. After the formation of a geoinformation model, modelling is performed using geographic information systems (GIS), information systems (IS, e.g. CAD), computing systems (CS).

The peculiarity of the result of geoinformation processing is that it has a digital and visual representation. Stages of geoinformation model formation , processing and result generation is controlled by a specialist (more often) and an operator (less often). When forming a geoinformation model , processing and generating the result the specialist uses a database of stereotypes or patterns. The final result of geoinformation processing is quality control. If the quality is low, the results are not accepted and the processing cycle is repeated. The generalised scheme of geoinformation processing is characterised by complexity, which is related to the processing technology.

The complexity chain in geoinformation technologies. Complexity theory and related concepts emerged in the mid to late 20th century in many disciplines, including the work of Prigogine and his study of dissipative structures in nonequilibrium thermodynamics, Lorenz in his study of weather systems and non-linear causal pathways, chaos theory and its new division of mathematics, and evolutionary thinking based on Lamarck's views on learning and adaptation [319].

The main type of modelling in geoinformation technologies is geoinformation modelling. Geoinformation modelling includes different types of modelling related to solving different tasks: electronic mapping, three-dimensional modelling of stationary objects, modelling in cadastre, design solutions in construction, monitoring of deformation and settlement of structures, transport monitoring, integration of remote sensing data. This determines the presence of complexity in geoinformation technologies and its diversity. Complexity in geographic information technologies and geographic information processing cannot be reduced to a single concept or parameter. Complexity in geoinformatics and geoinformation processing is a set of different types of complexity linked into a single system. Fig. 5.8 shows the chain of complexities that exist in geoinformatics. The technological links correspond to the types of complexity in Fig. 5.8. These types of complexity can be viewed as a system and as a network model or chain. If we consider the diagram in Fig. 5.8 as a system, it can be interpreted as a three-level system: input level: modelling level, experience level.

Figure 5.8. Chain of complexities included in the complexity of geoinformatics

Three related complexities are represented at the input level: structural complexity of a spatial object (or a connected system of objects); complexity of spatial object description (descriptive object model); complexity of decomposition of the spatial object description model into information units that serve as a basis for building a geoinformation or spatial model.

Decomposition is possible if there is an information language, syntax of model building, rules of using models, rules of their storage in the database and rules of visual representation of spatial models. The condition of decomposition is to ensure information correspondence between a spatial model and a spatial object.

A feature of the modelling level, including digital spatial modelling, is the dependence of the quality of work on the human operator. As such, three types of complexity: modelling complexity, design complexity, representation complexity 121

are related to the cognitive complexity of the operator. Cognitive complexity depends on the operator's experience, skills and ability to use spatial logic methods. Cognitive complexity is related to the accumulation of operating experience or accumulated reliability.

The level of experience accumulation includes: cognitive complexity; comparative complexity; the result of geoinformation modelling, accumulated quality. Geoinformation modelling solves the problems of spatial knowledge acquisition . Therefore, the result is

Geoinformatic modelling may be of technological and scientific interest as a means of developing technology and scientific direction of geoinformatics.

Geoinformation technology may include more than just geoinformation modelling. Auxiliary modelling in geoinformatics is logic modelling and logical spatial modelling. Auxiliary modelling is system modelling, structural modelling and reliability modelling. Auxiliary modelling is metamodelling, which serves as a basis for generalising experience and building metatheories. These are all part of the level of experience building and complexity reduction in geographic information technology.

Complexity in geographic information technology has similarities with Kolmogorov complexity, combinatorial complexity and complexity adaptive systems (CAS) [320]. Although there are a large number of CAS at different levels, complexity theory shows that there are common interrelated principles that can be observed in all CAS.

Factors of increasing and decreasing complexity in the actions of a specialist in geographic information technology. The term "complex" implies diversity through a large number and wide variety of interdependent but autonomous parts. "Adaptive" refers to the ability of a system to change, modify and learn from past experiences. The strengths of geoinformation technologies lie in the dependence on the relationships between the individual agents of the parts of the system (Figure 5.8) and their ability to self-organise. For this reason, the quality and analysis of the relationship between individual agents often determines the quality of the result of geoinformation technology, more than analysing the characteristics of individual agents. Nevertheless, agent performance is very important and needs to be investigated.

Often in works related to human-machine systems, the concept of an operator is introduced as a specially trained person to work with such systems. This operator blindly performs the task, not always clearly understanding the meaning of the task. In geographic information processing and geographic information systems, this concept should be replaced by the concept of "specialist". This is due to the fact that the functions of an operator when working with information and technical systems are performed by a subject matter expert. It should be noted that the number of such specialists working with geoinformation technologies is diverse: doctors, geodesists, geoinformaticians, cartographers, cadastre specialists, transport specialists, designers, surveyors and others. Fig. 5.9 shows the scheme of work of a specialist in geoinformation technologies, revealing the factors of emergence and complexity reduction.

Figure 5.9. Factors affecting complexity in geographic information technology.

In Figure 5.9, the STR symbols denote an "application specialist" who works using geographic information technology. This specialist has expertise that is most often expressed by the presence of tacit knowledge. The carrier of the tacit knowledge is the STR. The ROC symbol in Figure 5.9 denotes "quality of work result". It is possible to distinguish factors of direct proportion influencing the quality of work. Direct proportion relationships

The STR experience → quality of work result

GIS interface → quality of work result

Computing system performance quality →

quality of

work result

The quality of the processing task → the quality of the work result.

The experience of the STR affects the quality of the result of work using geoinformation technologies. The more experience, the higher the quality. The lower the experience of the GIS, the lower the quality. The interface of a GIS or other information system affects the quality of the work result. The more convenient the interface (Fig. 5.9) with many functions, the lower the complexity of work and the higher the quality. On the contrary, an uncomfortable interface increases the complexity of work and reduces the quality of the result.

High computing system performance reduces work time, simplifies modelling and ultimately improves the quality of the result of work. Low performance of the computing system increases work time, complicates modelling increases the complexity of work in geoinformation technologies and ultimately reduces the quality of the result of work

The quality of the processing task, if correctly and clearly defined, reduces the complexity and improves the quality of the work result. Low-quality processing task increases the complexity, creates additional work, creates loss of time, leads to increased fatigue and reduces the quality of the work result.

There are factors that increase the complexity of the work and decrease the quality of the work result. Formally, these factors are related to quality by the following paradigms.

Increasing data volume → decreasing quality of work result

Increase in cognitive complexity of processing → decrease in quality of work result

Increase in data processing time → decrease in the quality of the work result

The growth of data volume (Fig. 5.9) is an objective factor of recent times. It entails an increase in the complexity and decrease in the quality of work.

The increase in cognitive processing complexity is related to visual complexity and the increase in the number of relationships in the model or task (Figure 5.9).

A general conclusion can be drawn that complexity reduces the quality of the output in geographic information technology. This can be expressed by implicative models

Reducing complexity → improving quality

Increasing complexity → decreasing quality.

Implicative models are characterised by the situation of succession and the process of succession. These models are characterised by the situation of transformation of objects and models are characterised by the process of transformation. The process of abstraction is characteristic for implicative metamodels.

Different methods of complexity assessment are built on the basis of the underlying principles. Complexity assessment is based on the study of the relationships between models, the original object and the modelling result. The complexity assessment depends on the information situation. In different information situations, complexity has different types and is evaluated differently. Let us consider the example of digitalisation of maps.

A map, unlike a photograph, does not blindly copy reality, but is human-made and is a cartographic creative work. In cartography there is a concept of "exaggerated display" and shift. The task of the cartographer is to show "distinguishability" and "distinguishability". Exaggerated display is performed especially on small-scale maps (e.g. lakes), in order to distinguish the mapped object from a point. Distinguishability or shift is the spatial separation of objects on the map so that they do not merge into a single object. These include houses in dense urban areas and river embankments and riverbanks.

Therefore, when digitising maps, map objects cannot be blindly transferred into a digital map. This transformation must be done with the involvement of a specialist cartographer. This is an example of the cognitive complexity involved in working with certain types of spatial models. It must be remembered that a map primarily expresses qualitative features and secondarily quantitative features. A map primarily expresses topological relationships and secondarily geometric relationships. Therefore, map measurements or map numeration must be done with these factors in mind. This also sets the cognitive complexity.

In geoinformation technologies, as a rule, there is no central control mode. Control and information processing is carried out in the system through individual agents (specialists, operators). This allows the GIS system to respond and adapt more quickly and to a greater extent than if there were only one source of control.

Complexity in geoinformatics is a multidimensional phenomenon and manifests itself depending on the situation and the task assigned to the professional. Complexity in geoinformatics can be considered as a special type of complexity or as a complex complexity. Complexity in geoinformatics from a systemic perspective can be seen as a system of complexities or a chain of related complexities. The term "complex" implies diversity through a large number and great variety of interdependent but autonomous complex parts. The term "complex" implies not only difficulties, but also opportunities for adaptation in complex working conditions.

CHAPTER 6

6. Models in applied geoinformatics

6.1. Characteristics of geographic information models

Geoinformation models, like geodata, have three groups of characteristics (Figure 6.1): spatial (place); temporal (time); thematic (topic). Spatial characteristics define the position of the model in a certain coordinate system. These characteristics are associated with coordinate systems, so this group is often called coordinate. In addition, spatial characteristics are called metric characteristics because they allow various measurements and calculations. The main requirement for spatial characteristics is accuracy. This means that spatial characteristics define the position of a model in a coordinate system or relative to other models with a certain accuracy.

Fig.6.1 Main characteristics of data models in geoinformatics

Time characteristics define the time of obtaining the model construction or modelling time. They show the dependence of changes in the characteristics of the model (and object) with the passage of time. Temporal characteristics of the geographic information model [122] (GM) make it possible to study dynamic processes. They also make it possible to organise real-time control. The main requirement for temporal data is relevance. This means that the characteristics of the model are close to the characteristics of real objects at the current time. Irrelevant data is outdated data that cannot be applied in new changed conditions.

Thematic characteristics of the model describe characteristics of the GM that are not spatial or temporal. They include economic, statistical, technical, organisational, managerial and other types of characteristics. The main requirements for thematic data characteristics are completeness and representativeness. Completeness means that thematic data are sufficient for solving practical problems. Representativeness means that thematic data of the model fairly objectively reflect the relevant characteristics of the modelling object.

There are additional general characteristics of models, e.g., reliability, validity, etc. They are related to the quality of the model and do not apply to all groups. When processing and storing GMs, an important criterion for their use is stability or low variability. Among the three groups of GM characteristics, the coordinate data, "place" group has the highest stability. High stability of the coordinate group gives a reason to integrate the characteristics of models on the basis of the "place" group.

The other two groups of data are characterised by greater variability. According to this criterion, they are united into a single class called attributes (Fig. 6.1). Thus, the application of the stability criterion allows to categorise geodata into two groups.

A geographic information model is a unifying model. It includes all information from different collection technologies.

Its feature is that it contains a class of characteristics or data that is not explicitly present when the information is collected. This is associative data. Associative data provide the link between the visual representation of the model and its digital representation in the database. They serve as the basis for information processing in GIS.

Thus, the criterion of stability allows us to divide GM characteristics into two groups of "coordinate" and "attributive", and the *criterion of connectedness* allows us to form "associative" characteristics. There is a qualitative difference between them. The user works only with "coordinate" and "attribute" data, while "associative" data are embedded in the GIS mechanism and it operates with them.

6.2. Visual models

Graphical, cartographic and graphical forms of GM representation are called visual models. Visual models can be represented using computer graphics and, if necessary, converted into paper originals. Visual geoinformation models serve as a basis for spatial analysis. Their structure is shown in Fig. 6.2. Graphical data can have vector or raster representation. Vector data may or may not contain information about object topology.

Topology defines the relationships between parts of a model or between models. For example, the confluence of two rivers has one kind of topological relationship and the intersection of a street has another. Two roads may intersect or pass one over the other. The vector non-topological form of representing an object answers the question, "*Where is the object located ?*". A vector topological form of representation answers the questions: "*Where is the object located ? What connections with other objects does it have?*" (Fig.6.2.).

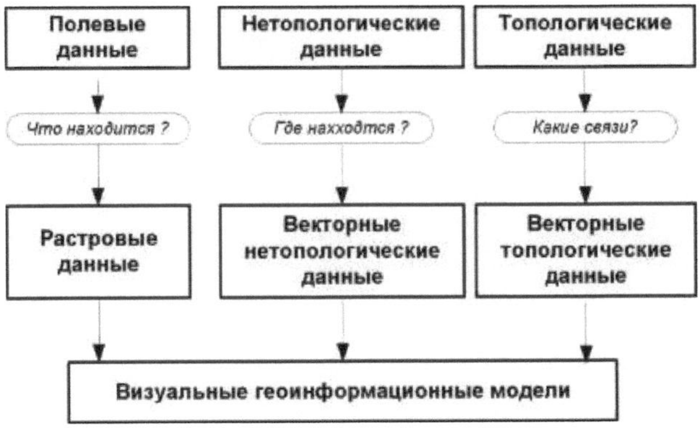

Fig. 6.2. Structure of graphical data

Geoinformation models must necessarily have topological characteristics. Topology definition is fixed semantically during metric information collection. Topology input is performed on the basis of semantic modelling after metric information collection.

There is a qualitative difference between vector and raster representations of models in geoinformatics. Raster data represent data fields and are field-based. They represent objects and the background on which the objects are located. Geographic information systems that use raster models as the main source of information are called field-based systems.

Vector models in applied geoinformatics represent spatial contour or linear objects and vector spatial fields. They have an object-based nature. Therefore, geographic information systems that use vector models as the main source of information are called object-based.

Raster models in applied geoinformatics represent spatial areal objects and vector areal or mass spatial fields. Raster models are obtained by scanning. They characterise the field form of the models. For further information processing the raster form of models is converted into vector form of the same models. Conversion from raster form to vector form means transition from field representation of models to object representation of models. At transition from raster form to vector form selection (selection of characteristics of a certain type) and essential (100-1000 times) reduction of geoinformation model volume is carried out, but with preservation of informativeness [322, 322] of spatial objects description.

Raster-vector transformation (vectorisation) is applied in interpretation of scanned aerospace images, in methods of raster cartographic images processing, in processing of data received from digital cameras, etc. The form of representation for attribute data is descriptive. In general, there are the following forms of geodata representation: analytical (formulas, functions), topological (graphs); graphical (charts, figures); tabular (tables); textual; cartographic.

For processing in information and geoinformation systems, attribute data are converted into a table form of representation. A table containing attributes of objects is called an attribute table. In it each object corresponds to a row of the table, each thematic attribute corresponds to a column of the table. The use of tables is also dictated by the fact that the table is the basic model in relational databases.

The temporal form can be reflected in several ways: fixing in one table or in several tables the attributes of a given object for different time stages; specifying the time period of objects' existence; correlating the collected information with certain moments of time; specifying the speed of objects' movement.

6.3. Classes of coordinate models

All coordinate models use the characteristics of "place". However, there is a qualitative difference between them that allows them to be categorised into classes of coordinate models. One of the main purposes of coordinate models is to represent spatial properties of objects. Spatial objects have a certain shape, which requires an information correspondence between the shape of the model and the shape of the object.

The analysis of spatial objects allows us to divide them into the following classes: sets of individual localised objects; sets of linear and network objects; sets of area (areal) objects. These classes of spatial objects serve as a basis for the organisation of three classes of geoinformation models (Fig. 6.3).

In informational correspondence with the grouping of spatial objects in geoinformatics the main classes of models are used: point, linear and areal models. Point models represent separately located objects. Linear models represent lines or contours (areal boundaries). Areal models represent territories. In some systems, the description of the basic model types includes the concept of *a spatial network*, which is an extension of the *neighbourhood* data type. Contours and lines are often combined by the common term "linear objects". Thus, the number of main classes of coordinate models varies from three to five in different GIS.

Point models. *Point geoinformation* models are a class of models that represent spatial objects localised in a small part of space.

Point models contain two main properties and answer two questions.

They show ***where*** an object is located, for example, in a geographic coordinate system.
They give a brief characterisation of the object and show ***what kind of*** object it is.

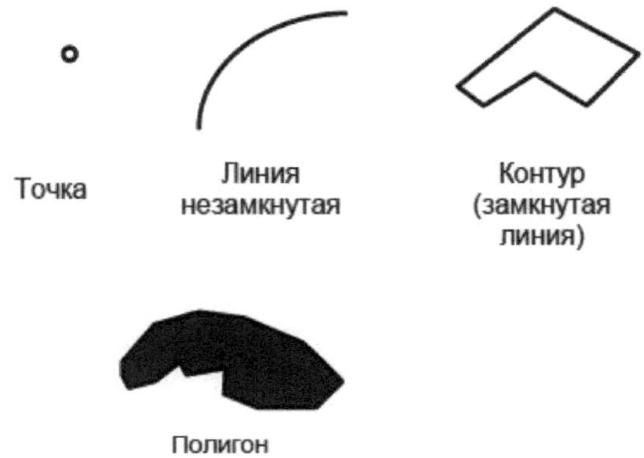

Fig.6.3 Types of spatial object models

Point models do not define the dimensions of an object. but their location. This type of model includes all point symbols. The choice of objects represented as points depends on the scale of the map or survey. For example, on a large-scale map, point models show individual buildings, and on a small-scale map, point models show cities. Point geo-information models can be stored in two forms: as graphic files, like other spatial objects; as tables, like attributes. The latter is due to the fact that point models are always characterised by only two coordinates. Therefore, information about point models can always be stored as a table containing the same number of columns.

In addition to coordinates, this table may contain identification numbers, thematic characteristics, etc. In such tables, each row corresponds to one point model - it contains all information. Each column is a feature containing typified data: coordinates or attributes. Each point is independent of all other points represented by individual rows. Point models have no topological characteristics. The information unit of a point model - a point is a mathematical abstraction and serves as a basis for localisation.

Linear models. *Linear geoinformation* models are a class of models that represent spatial extended objects using lines or networks. This model is formed by a set of connected lines, which determines its name. Linear models answer the following questions.

1. 0 they show ***where the*** object is located, for example, in a geographic coordinate system.

2. They show ***what kind of*** object it is and give a brief characterisation of the object.

3. They show ***what the linear dimensions of*** the object are.

4. They show ***in what relationship*** an object is in relation to other objects

Linear geoinformation models are characterised by the presence of topological features. Any linear model consists of nodes (vertices) and lines (arcs). For each node there is a topological feature called *valence*, defined by the number of line segments intersecting in it. For example, the ends of isolated lines are univalent. For street networks (cross-type intersections), quadrivalent nodes are most characteristic. In hydrology, trivalent nodes are most common.

In the hierarchical model, each pair of nodes has only one connection, no loops or closed loops are allowed. This model describes part of the river networks (without islands). The presence of islands requires a network model.

Linear objects, like point objects, have their own attributes, and they are different for arcs (links) and nodes. For point objects it is necessary to specify one coordinate value, for linear objects - at least two (for the start and end points). In a more general case the number of points in a linear model is arbitrary. Information unit of linear model - *line* serves as a basis for creation of vector models.

Areal models. *Areal geoinformation* models are a class of models that represent spatial objects with closed boundaries and presence of some properties inside these boundaries. Areal models answer the following questions.

1. 0 they show ***where the*** object is located, for example, in a geographic coordinate system.

2. They show ***what kind of*** object it is and give a brief characterisation of the object.

3. They show ***what the linear dimensions of*** the object are.

4. They show ***what the area dimensions of*** the object are.

5. They show ***what the properties of*** the object's ***boundaries are.***

6. They show ***what the properties of an object are*** inside the boundaries.

7. They show ***in what relationship*** an object is in relation to other objects

Areal models answer more questions and are the most informative of the coordinate models. Areal models, like linear models, can have topological characteristics. In areal models, boundaries can be defined by a property or phenomenon, as well as independently of the phenomenon. Boundaries may correspond to the boundaries of a spatial feature (state boundary), a phenomenon (flood or fire zone) or be artificially established (e.g., for

neighbourhoods).
Each of the models has its own information unit. For point models, the information unit is a point. For linear models, the information unit is a line segment. The information unit of an areal model is an area unit. In raster models and images the information unit of areal model is a *pixel.* It serves as a basis for building areal models of any shape.

6.4. Accuracy of geoinformation models

The use of any information is acceptable if it fulfils certain criteria and standards. One of the criteria for the applicability of spatial and temporal data in geoinformatics is accuracy.
Accuracy is defined as - the closeness of results, calculations or estimates to true values or values assumed to be true. For example, the accuracy of a horizon obtained after digitalisation or scanning can be assessed by comparing it with the horizon on the original map. Let us consider several indicators of accuracy in geographic information models: accuracy of calculation, accuracy of measurement, accuracy of representation.
The accuracy of the calculation is determined by the number of significant digits after the decimal point,
The accuracy of measurements is determined by the number of significant digits in the measurements
The accuracy of the representation is determined by the number of digits describing the coordinate data.
The term "significant" digits means that the digit carries useful information. For example, you can calculate a number with 20 decimal places in a calculation. But if the calculation algorithm creates an error in the third decimal place, it makes no sense to write all the digits after the second decimal place. The accuracy of a calculation is usually higher than the accuracy of a measurement. Accuracy is part of the data complex, which defines an important indicator - data quality.
Positional accuracy is expressed as the degree of deviation of the location data from the true position of the object on the ground. Typically, map accuracy is roughly defined by line thickness or 0.4 mm. This corresponds to 10m at a scale of 1:25,000.
The accuracy of attributes is determined by the closeness of the attribute values to its true value. Attributes may change more frequently over time compared to coordinate data.

6.5. Topological models

Topological models are a broader concept than vector models in geoinformatics. The simplest ideas of topology arise from direct observation of the world around us. The ideas and methods of topology are of theoretical and practical interest for geoinformatics. The description of spatial properties of real world objects is not exhausted by information about their "metric" characteristics. For example, an ordinary line describing some spatial object may be closed or not closed; may or may not intersect with another line; may or may not form nodes. Bodies, their surfaces, may have "holes".

Topological properties of spatial objects are those that do not change under any deformations made without breaks or connections. Besides elementary geometrical figures, many mathematical objects have topological properties. The first important observations and exact topological relations were found as early as Euler, Gauss and Riemann. Topology as a section of science was founded in the late 19th century by A. Poincaré. The basic idea of topology is the idea of continuity. It is also found in mathematical analysis. The idea of continuity receives its full and comprehensive development in topology.

A large number of spatial objects in geoinformatics have a variety of spatial connections and relations. This leads to the need to specify a topological description of objects. In these cases, topological models are used to describe such objects.

Topological models are models that reflect mutual relationships between objects that are independent of the morphological properties of the objects.

Fig. 6.4 shows topologically related models. These models (figures) have the same topology - the same topological properties.

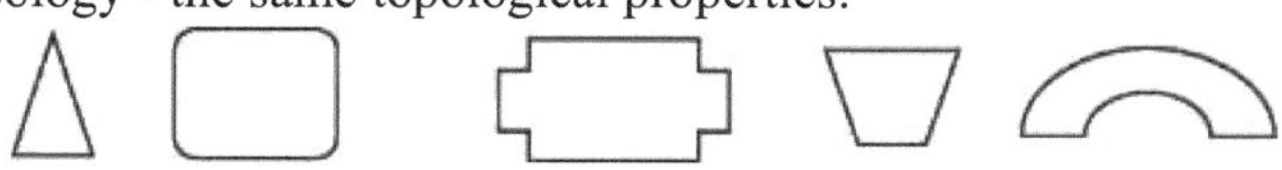

Figure 6.4. Topologically related figures

Another example of topologically related figures can be arithmetic signs of addition " + " and multiplication " x ". Graphical models of geoinformatics differ significantly from CAD models by their topological characteristics. This difference can be seen in the software and hardware of these systems. Topological models allow to represent map elements and the whole map as a set of graphs. The theoretical basis of topological models are algebraic topology and graph theory. According to algebraic topology, the coordinate data types: areas, lines and points are called 2-cells, 1-cells and 0-cells respectively. A map is considered as an oriented two-dimensional cell complex.

Topological features should be calculated during quantitative transformations of object models and then stored in the database 138 data together with coordinate data. In geoinformatics, a topological model is defined by the presence of the following characteristics. Connectivity of vectors - contours, roads and other vectors should be stored not as independent sets of points, but as interconnected objects (Fig. 6.5).

Figure 6.5 Topological properties: connectedness, adjacency and proximity 8.

Neighbourhood connectivity and adjacency - information about the mutual location of neighbourhoods and neighbourhood interruption nodes (Fig. 6.5);
Proximity - an indicator of spatial proximity of linear or areal objects (Fig. 6.5), evaluated by a numerical parameter, in this case symbol 8.
Intersection - information on intersection types allows to reproduce bridges and road intersections (Fig. 6.6). Thus L-shaped intersection (2 lines) is bivalent; T-shaped intersection (3 lines) is trivalent; and X-shaped (4 lines) is called quadrivalent;

Fig.6.6 Intersections: bivalent, trivalent and quadrivalent.

Topological characteristics of linear objects can be represented visually using connected graphs. A graph preserves the structure of the model with all nodes and intersections. It resembles a map with distorted scale. An example of such a graph is an underground scheme. The difference between an underground map and an underground diagram reflects the difference between a map and a graph.
Nodes of the graph describing the cartographic model correspond to road crossings, places where roads meet bridges, road junctions, etc. The edges of such a graph describe road sections and objects connecting them. In this model, the length of edges may not carry informative load. Topological characteristics

of areal objects are represented using two types of graphs: coverage and adjacency.

Topologisation - procedure of introducing topological properties into vector models. As a special case **topologisation is** transformation of a linear vector model of "*spaghetti*" type (Fig. 6.7a) into a *topological* model (Fig. 6.76)

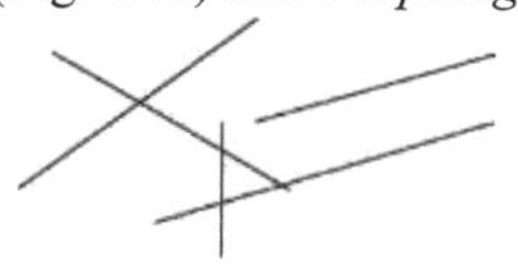

a

Fig. 6.7 Vector model of "spaghetti" type a), vector topological model b)

Spaghetti type vector model represents a set of unconnected linear objects superimposed on each other without specifying and taking into account their intersection and joints. It is obtained by automated vectorisation and when linear objects have no topological characteristics. In contrast to this model, vector topological model (Fig.6.7b) takes into account topological properties, namely connectivity of linear objects, indication of their intersection and joint points.

In Fig. 6.7b intersections are marked by points (nodes). The theoretical basis of topological models is algebraic topology and graph theory. According to algebraic topology, the coordinate data types: areas, lines and points are called 2-cells, 1-cells and 0-cells respectively. A map is considered as an oriented two-dimensional cell complex.

Topological characteristics are stored in the database together with coordinate data. Topological characteristics of linear objects can be represented visually using connected graphs. A graph preserves the structure of the model with all nodes and intersections. It resembles a map with a distorted scale. An example of such a graph is an underground scheme. The distinction between an underground map and an underground scheme reflects the difference between a metric spatial model - a map - and a topological non-metric model - a graph. Topological characteristics of areal objects are represented by means of graphs of two types: coverage and adjacency.

The coverage graph of spatial objects is a model that simplistically represents the real location of objects. We can say that the coverage graph corresponds to the visible spatial reality.

The coverage graph of area objects corresponds (topologically homomorphic) to the contour map of corresponding districts. The edges of such a graph describe the boundaries between the districts, and its nodes represent the points of connection of districts. The degree of a vertex of such a graph is the number of districts that interconnect in it.

The adjacency graph of spatial objects is a model that represents the relationships between spatial objects. We can say that the adjacency graph corresponds to the connections of spatial reality. This model is artificial, its purpose is to spatially analyse the connections between objects.

An adjacency graph is a coverage graph turned inside out. In it, neighbourhoods are represented by nodes and a pair of adjacent neighbourhoods by edges. On the basis of such a graph it is possible to answer the question whether the area under consideration is passable, divided into passable or impassable areas. Topological characteristics are accompanied by positional and descriptive information.

At the first stage of building geoinformation models, linear and area objects are built. After that, the topology is "created". These processes include calculating and encoding relationships between points, lines and areas.

Intersections and links have vector representation. Topological characteristics are recorded during data encoding as additional attributes. This process is done automatically in many GIS during the digitalisation of (cartographic or photogrammetric) data.

Objects are connected by a set of relations between them. In turn, relations define sets of links. The simplest examples of such relations are: "nearest to ...", "intersects", "connected to ...". Each object can be assigned a feature, which is an identifier of the nearest object of the same class; in this way the relations between pairs of objects are encoded.

6.6. Vector models

Geoinformation models can have *vector* or *raster* (mesh) representation, contain or not contain topological characteristics. This approach allows classifying graphical models into three types: raster model; vector non-topological model; vector topological model. All these models are mutually transformable.

Vector data models are built on lines that occupy a part of space in contrast to raster models that occupy the whole space. This determines their main advantage - they require orders of magnitude less memory for storage and less time for processing and representation. Vector models are created by connecting points by straight lines, arcs, polylines. Square objects in vector models are defined by sets of lines.

In reality, one deals not with abstract lines and points, but with objects containing lines and ranges, occupying a spatial position, and with complex relationships between them. Therefore, a complete vector data model depicts

spatial data as a set of the following main parts:
geometric (metric) objects (points, lines and polygons);
attributes - attributes associated with objects;
connections between objects.

Vector models display all types of coordinate models: point, line, area. These types of coordinate models are defined through the information unit *line* as follows. A point is defined as a line of zero length. A line is defined as a line of finite length. An area is represented by a sequence of interconnected linear segments.

Vector models are obtained in different ways. One of the most common is vectorisation of scanned (raster) images. It consists in extraction of vector objects from scanned image and obtaining them in vector format. Another way is to build a model in the editing mode.

Some objects are vector objects by definition, e.g., roads, boundaries of the relevant land parcel, district boundaries, etc. Therefore, vector models are usually used to collect data on boundaries and long linear or network objects. Analysis and design operations are easier to perform in vector form. For example, network analysis, development of traffic routes on the road network, traffic intensity analysis, etc.

In raster formats, a point object must occupy an entire cell. This creates a number of difficulties related to the ratio of image size to object size.

As for accuracy of vector data, it is possible to speak about advantage of vector models over raster ones, because vector data can be encoded with any conceivable degree of accuracy, which is limited only by possibilities of the method of internal coordinates representation. Usually 8 or 16 decimal places (single or double precision) are used to represent vector data.

Only some classes of data obtained from measurement correspond to the accuracy of vector data. These are data obtained by precise surveying (coordinate geometry); maps of small areas made from topographic coordinates and political boundaries defined by precise surveying.

Not all natural phenomena have characteristic clear boundaries that can be represented as mathematically defined lines. This is due to the dynamics of the phenomena or the way spatial information is collected. Soils, vegetation types, slopes, wildlife habitat - all these objects do not have clear boundaries.

6.7. Raster models

Raster models are spatial models describing spatial reality, in which the whole object (the territory under study) is mapped discretely into an areal. Representation of models on the computer screen is always raster, regardless of whether the initial model is raster or vector. It is reasonable to compare vector and raster models. In both models there are point, linear and area objects. Fig. 6.9 shows point elements of vector and raster models.

Fig.6.8. Point elements of vector and raster model.

The basic element (information unit) of a vector model is a line, and a mathematical point, which, although displayed by some designation, has no geometric dimensions. The basic element (information unit) of a raster model is a pixel, which has quite certain dimensions and occupies a certain area of space.

The basic element of a vector model has coordinates measured on an interval scale. This means that the neighbourhood of one point can be as close as desired to the neighbourhood of another point. Points can be close or distant by any distance.

The basic element of the raster model has coordinates measured in integer scale. This means that neighbouring points can be either neighbours (Fig.6.9) or separated by a distance multiple of an integer number of pixels. In Fig.6.9 the basic element of the raster model is shown in light colour and its fixed neighbourhood in dark colour.

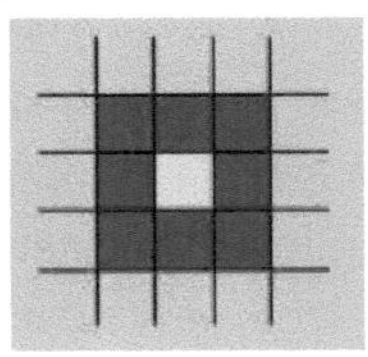

Fig.6.9 Pixel neighbourhood in integer coordinate system.

Comparison of linear raster and vector objects also emphasises the difference between them. Fig.6.10. shows straight line segments for raster and for vector model.

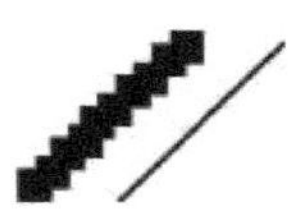

Fig.6.10. Line segments in raster and vector images

It should be noted that the image, if it is located not strictly vertically or horizontally forms a stepped figure having thickness and "roughness". At scaling (for example, at enlargement) of such figures the following happens.

A vector line may increase in length, but its thickness as a mathematical object will remain unchanged. Regardless of the scale, a vector segment is expressed as two points: the beginning and the end.

The raster line will increase in both length and width. This is because the number of pixels that form it has also increased. The most unpleasant is the

distortion caused by the element of random addition of a pixel on one side and disappearance of a pixel on the other side. As a result, a scaled raster figure may not be similar to itself at a smaller scale. This effect is especially noticeable at the intersection of straight lines.
In addition, there is a difference in the measurement of vector and raster line lengths. The length of a vector line is measured using the Cartesian metric or simplified as the Pythagorean distance, while the length of a stepped raster line is defined as the length of steps or the Manhattan distance. For example, for a triangle with sides 3x3 linear units, the Pythagorean distance (hypotenuse) will be 4.2426 and the Manheton distance will be 6 linear units.
Comparison of areal raster and vector objects also emphasises the difference. Figure 6.11 shows two triangles in vector and raster forms. Significant shape distortion can be seen in the raster figure.

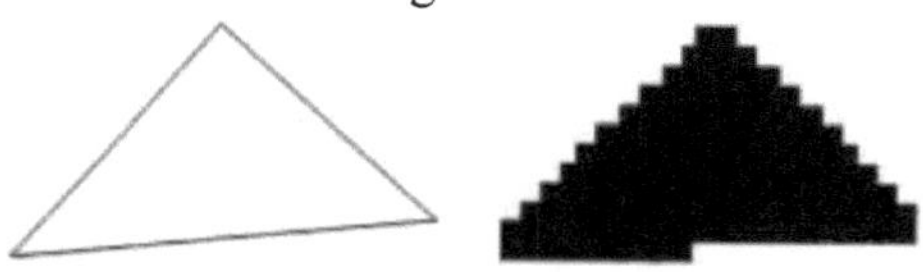

Fig.6.11. Areal objects in vector and raster forms
In practice, pixel sizes are chosen to be so small that a visual distinction such as that shown in Fig. 6.11 becomes imperceptible. But it is fundamental that the noted effects are preserved. Since the image is formed on the basis of equal intervals, it refers to regular patterns or regular networks.
A regular network is a set of regular geometrical figures: squares, triangles, etc. Each cell of the raster model corresponds to the same size but different in characteristics (colour, density) area (pixel). Each cell represents a real surface area, which is also characterised by colour characteristics. However, a cell of the raster model contains a single value that summarises the colour and light characteristics of the real surface area. In image processing theory, this procedure is known as pixelisation.
If a vector model provides information about ***where*** this or that object is located, a raster model provides information about ***what is*** located at this or that point in the territory. This determines the main purpose of raster models - continuous representation of the surface. An ordered set of pixnlnels forms a raster.
Bitmaps allow you to display halftones. As a rule, each raster element or each cell should have a single density and/or colour value. For example, when the boundary of two types of coatings may pass through the centre of a raster element, the element is given a value that describes the larger part of the cell or its centre point. A number of systems allow multiple values for a single

image element. Fig.6.12 shows three vector objects: line, ellipse and arc.

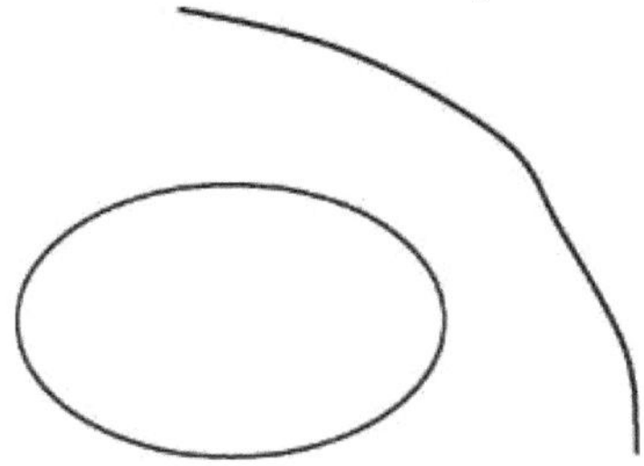

Fig.6.12. Initial vector objects

Fig. 6.13 shows raster images of the objects of Figure 6.12. As can be seen from these figures, the raster image "coarsens" the original vector object. The difference between them is that the raster object is measured in integer coordinates, while the vector object is measured in ordinary Cartesian coordinates, more precisely in the interval scale. That is why the accuracy of vector objects definition is fundamentally higher. On the other hand, the speed of integer variables processing is higher than interval variables.

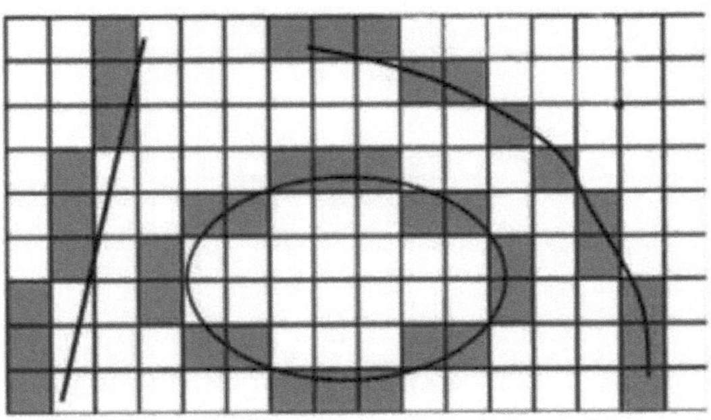

Fig. 6.13. Raster images of source objects

Formation of the raster model is shown in Fig. 6.14. 6.14. The initial image (snapshot) has a continuous distribution (Fig. 6.14a) of density D along some direction L. This model is called analogue because it is described by the dependence $D=f(L)$

Fig. 6.14 b shows the digitising process. The curve is divided into equal segments equal to the pixel size. In the centre of each segment the average density (value) for this pixel is calculated.

Fig. 6.14c shows the result of the digitising process - a raster model. In this section it represents a histogram. On the basis of the analysis we can give the following definition of a bitmap model

Density Analogue model

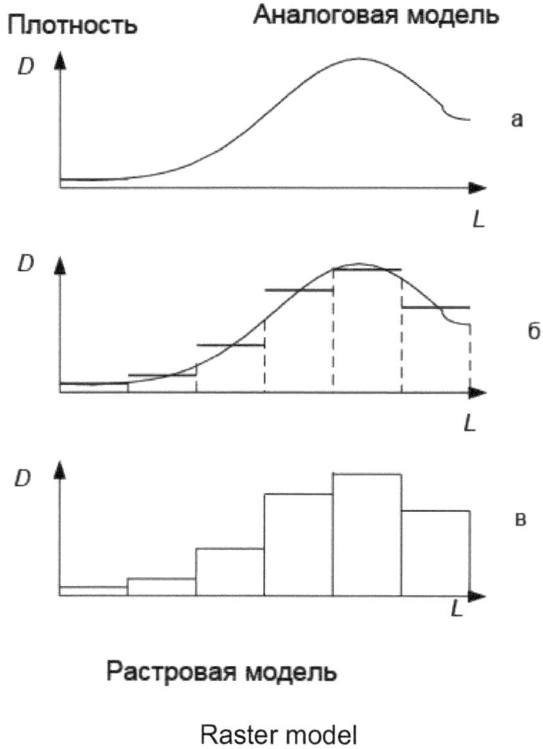

Fig. 6.14. Raster model formation

Raster model - regular digital model of image density represented in integer coordinate system. The term digital image is widely used in photogrammetry and in scanner image processing.

6.8. Characteristics of raster models.

There are a number of characteristics for raster models: resolution, orientation, zones, value, position.

Resolution - the minimum linear size of the smallest area of a real surface displayed by a single pixel.

Pixels are usually rectangles or squares, less often triangles and hexagons are used. Higher resolution has a raster with smaller cell size. High resolution implies: abundance of details, many cells, minimum cell size.

Value - information element stored in an image element (pixel). Since typed data is used during processing, it is necessary to define types of raster model values.

The *type of values* in the cells of the image is determined both by the real phenomenon and by the specifics of the GIS. In particular, different classes of values can be used in different systems: integers, real (decimal) values, letter values.
The integers may be optical density characteristics or codes indicating the position in the accompanying table or legend. For example, the following legend indicating the name of the soil class is possible: 0 - empty class, 1 - loamy, 2 - sandy, 3 - crushed stone, etc.
Orientation - the angle between the north direction and the position of the image columns.
Raster model *zone* - neighbouring cells with the same value and representing one phenomenon or object. A zone can be separate objects, natural phenomena, areas of soil types, elements of hydrography, etc.
A buffer zone is an auxiliary zone that is built around point, linear or areal objects based on a given rule or fixed value. The main characteristics of the zone are its value and position. Figure 6.15 shows buffer zones for areal and linear objects. The objects are highlighted in a different colour.

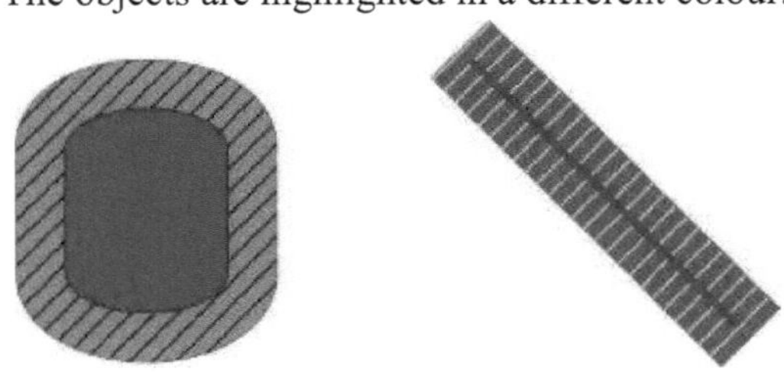

Figure 6.15. Buffer zones for areal and linear facilities.

The *position* is usually given by an ordered pair of coordinates (row number and column number), which uniquely define the position of each element of the mapped space in the image.
Comparing vector and raster models, we should note the convenience of vector models for organising and working with interrelations of objects. Nevertheless, using simple techniques, for example, including interrelations in attribute tables, it is possible to organise interrelations in raster systems as well. It is especially effective to calculate area in raster systems. It is necessary to stop on questions of display accuracy in raster models. In raster formats in most cases it is not clear whether coordinates refer to the central point of a pixel or to one of its corners. That is why the accuracy of raster element binding is defined as 1/2 of cell width and height.
Raster models have the following d o s t r a t i o n s :
raster does not require preliminary acquaintance with the phenomena, data are

collected from a uniformly located network of points, which allows to further obtain objective characteristics of the investigated objects on the basis of statistical methods of processing. Due to this, raster models can be used to study new phenomena about which no material has been accumulated. Due to its simplicity, this method is the most widespread;

raster data are easier to process by parallel algorithms and thus provide higher performance compared to vector data;

Some tasks, such as creating a buffer zone or calculating habitat area, are much easier to solve in raster form;

many raster models allow to input vector data, while the reverse procedure is very difficult for vector models;

rasterisation processes are algorithmically simpler than vectorisation processes, which often require expert decisions.

Most often raster models are used in the processing of aerospace images to obtain remote sensing data.

6.9. Digital spatial models

The development of automated methods of information processing has led to the emergence of a new trend in modelling - digital modelling and special models called digital models. The term "digital modelling" is a synonym of the term "computer modelling". Digitizing (digitizing, digitising, digitalisation) - information technology for converting analogue data into a discrete (digital) form suitable for use in computer technologies.

The term "digital" is borrowed from the name "digital computing machines" (DCMs). In the early stages of development of computer technology there were two types of computing machines analogue and digital. Analogue (AVMs) processed continuous analogue signals. They used specially designed electronic circuits in which functional transformation of analogue information was carried out. The transient characteristic of such a circuit corresponded to the required processing algorithm.

Digital computers were based on the conversion of analogue signals into discrete sequences while retaining information. In order to process information with the help of a digital computer it must be digitalised (digtal - digital), i.e. converted into a digital code. It is the digital code that is the dominant factor determining the essence of the term "digital". In operation, it turned out that digital machines were more versatile, as they allowed processing different sets of data with different programmes. They were also cheaper in terms of production cost. Versatility and low cost were significant competitive advantages of digital machines over analogue machines, which led to the displacement of AVMs.

Nowadays, analogue computing machines are used as special processors. The term "digital means that the information in these data and systems is contained in discrete form and is designed to be processed using modern technology.

In a broad sense, a digital model *(DM)* is a discrete model formed: for transmission in communication systems, for storage in a database, for processing on a computer. Digital spatial model (DM) in geoinformatics is a computer-oriented model.

Digital models can be stored in databases or as file structures. Digital spatial models are most widely used in geoinformatics, design, construction, architecture, ecology, etc. Digital models contain different types of information (Fig. 6.16). According to the aspect of spatial relations, metric and attributive types of information are distinguished. Semantic and syntactic components are distinguished according to the aspect of semiotic analysis.

Metric information defines position by specifying coordinates of DEM points and object dimensions by relative coordinates of points in conventional or local systems.

The qualitative difference between the metric information of digital models derived from real measurements is the accuracy characteristic. It is caused by measurement errors and subsequent calculation errors. This parameter determines the applicability of a digital model in solving practical problems at different scales.

Attributive information in DEM defines belonging of points or objects to a certain class or object (complex or simple object), describes properties of objects and their parts, defines interrelations and conditions of processing, conditions of reproduction, etc. As well as in all geoinformatics it solves the main task of finding spatial relations

The semiotic aspect allows, considering the CM as an information model, to introduce the estimates of the informativeness coefficient and meaningfulness coefficient of the digital model known in informatics.

Semantic part of information defines its content side, it is related to data encoding. *Syntactic information* defines a set of rules for working with a digital model as with an ordinary information model. It is related to classification and rules of model construction.

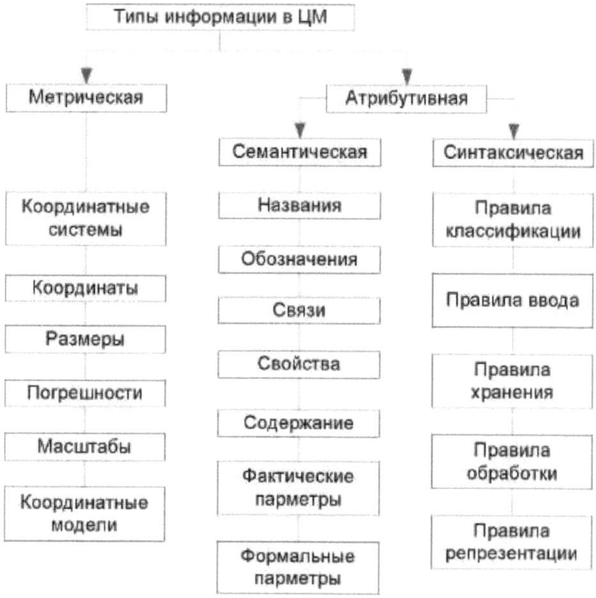

Fig. 6.16. Types of information in a digital model

The logical structure of DEM is defined as a set of schemes and logical records describing the given DEM. It may include schemes of interrelation of parts of DEM in nature, in database, schemes of interrelation of DEM properties and schemes of DEM construction. It contains logical records that constitute the information basis. A logical record is an element of the logical structure of the DEM.

The physical structure of the DEM is determined by the way of realisation of the logical DEM on a particular technical basis. It defines the format of data record, sizes of clusters, words, etc. The element of the physical structure of the DEM is the physical record. These two parts are the correspondence of the datalogical and physical models. Thus, the digital model is a model combining the datalogical and physical models.

Among spatial digital models there are several: digital terrain model, digital object model, digital model of a phenomenon (process) Let us consider them as an example. The digital terrain model is the most widely used in CAD and geoinformatics.

A digital terrain model *(DTM)* represents terrain objects and contains information about the terrain in the form of discrete data sets. *A digital* terrain *model* (DTM) is an information discrete terrain model intended for storage and processing in computer technologies, which should contain several basic properties derived from its definition, namely:

1. As an information model, the DEM should contain complete (within the framework of solved tasks) information about the modelling object. In this part we can talk about the semantic component of the DEM.

2. As a semiotic model, the CMM includes three parts:

- syntax - rules of construction and usage;
- semantics - the meaningful part about the modelling object;
- pragmatics - to be useful, to have a measure of utility.

3. As digital, it must be optimally organised and convenient to work on a computer. It must be represented in digital code on a machine-readable medium.

4. As a model in general, the DEM must be classified on a known class of models.

5. As a model of an object the DEM should contain special thematic information about the modelled object.

6. As a database model, the DEM should be organised in a way that does not take the form of a database structure.

7. As an information product, the DEM should have consumer properties.

One of the varieties of DEM is a digital elevation model. This model is used to represent the terrain relief. One of the ways to solve this problem is to use isolines. *Isolines are* lines that represent spatial lines corresponding to equal value of some value distributed in space. For example, it can be lines of equal heights (*horizontals*) on the terrain or lines characterising the depth of a water body (isobaths from iso ... and Greek bathos - depth), etc.). Figure 6.17 shows a digital elevation model in the form of isolines.

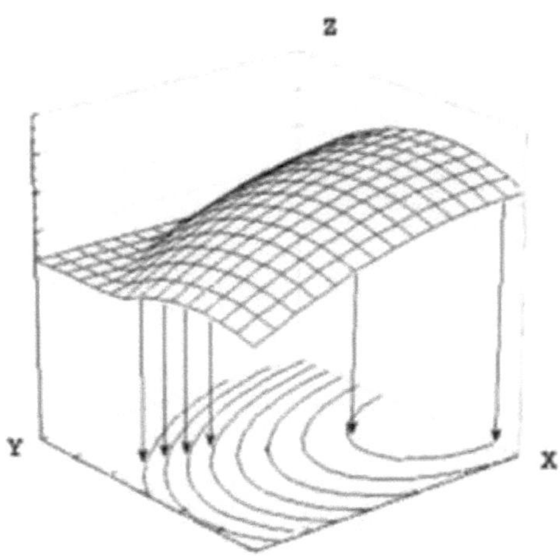

Fig. 6.17. Isolines - lines in the plane as lines of equal heights

Digital object model (DEM) - information discrete model of an object intended for storage and processing in computer technologies. It includes a set of coordinates of points characterising the object, connections between points, information about object properties

A digital phenomenon model (DPM) is a discrete model of a spatial phenomenon, designed for storage and processing in computer technologies Its peculiarity is that it is formed in the form of data sets forming a time series. This makes it possible to monitor and make predictive assessments. Similarly to a DEM, a DEM can be depicted in the form of various isolines describing different processes and phenomena.

CHAPTER 7

7. Spatial logic in applied geoinformatics.

Applied geoinformatics studies space and logically analyses spatial objects and processes. As such, it is related to spatial logic. Applied geoinformatics uses and develops spatial logic [323]. It can be argued that after geometry, spatial logic is most clearly developed in applied geoinformatics.

Spatial logic [324-327] is a direction in logical reasoning, which is not so much related to logic as to spatial and abstract images. Therefore, it can be argued that spatial logic in applied geoinformatics is the logic of images and image constructions.

Spatial logic in applied geoinformatics is developing in two directions. The first direction can be called "logical". It is connected with verification of validity and non-contradiction of spatial constructions.

The second direction should be called the direction of supporting the methods of other sciences. For example, in photogrammetry, spatial logic allows to improve photogrammetric constructions [328] and to obtain new solutions to spatial problems. In the field of land use, spatial logic allows to obtain new methods of area estimation [329] for land plots of arbitrary shape. In essence, this approach uses a synthesis of probabilistic logic [330] and spatial logic.

Spatial logic is used in heuristic methods for solving the problem of location or site selection. An example is the selection of a landing site for returning spacecraft. [331].

Spatial logic is applied in the analysis of visual models.

In particular. when analysing the semantics of visual models [332] and analysing their informativeness [333].

In spatial management of moving objects, there is a need to apply the cognitive resources of the manager [334]. In this case, spatial logic is combined with the application of cognitive logic [335]

Spatial logic is closely related to spatial reasoning [336], to visual modelling with geoinformatics. Spatial logic is applied in knowledge extraction and ontology analysis [337]. Spatial logic is applied in computational processes in the organisation of parallel computing. Spatial logic is applied in analysing computer reasoning schemes related to spatial domains such as robotics and technical vision [338].

Spatial logic is used in interactive information processing using geographic information systems. Spatial logic in the aspect of spatial thinking and perception is used in psychology as a method of spatial thinking and perception of the world. The language of spatial logic is a formal language [324] interpreted over a class of structures representing real objects, geometric objects and spatial relations. Such a formal language can use any logical syntax: the syntax of first-order logic, some fragment of first-order logic, or possibly higher-order logic. The structures over which it is interpreted can reside in any class of geometric "spaces": topological spaces, affine spaces, projective spaces, in Euclidean 3-dimensional space. There can be as many spatial languages as there are kinds of spatial logics. Therefore, spatial logics can be considered as

family of spatial logics.

7.1. Types of spatial logic.

Spatial logic includes several parts: geometric logic, topological logic, set-theoretic logic, image logic (spatial diagrams or spatial images), visual positioning (the field of vision [338] and artificial intelligence), spatial knowledge acquisition (the field of artificial intelligence). Common to spatial logics is that the logical concept of reality depends on the underlying geometry of structures and axioms. Spatial logics are applied in education where they interface with cognitive representations. Spatial logic is applied in virtual simulation, where it relies on the logic of behaviour in real space. Summarising the applications of spatial logic, its importance for artificial intelligence methods should be noted, as it allows modelling reasoning that can be used in intelligent systems.

Geometric logic. Geometric logic includes: definitions; postulates; and theorems; target statements (problems) that need to be proved or constructed using some standard logical inference mechanism. Such a scheme of knowledge acquisition from images is reproduced by logic programming systems, including geometric inference systems. In automated image processing, construction tasks correspond to latent analysis tasks, and proof tasks correspond to object recognition tasks

The logic of Euclid's plane geometry does not allow the intersection of parallel lines. In this geometry, a triangle in the plane always has a sum of interior angles equal only to l. The logic of geometry on the sphere excludes the notion of a straight line and replaces it with the notion of a geodesic line. The logic of geometry on the sphere admits the termination of parallel lines. The logic of geometry on the sphere admits the sum of interior angles equal to 3/2 *p*

Thus, geometric logic is given by basic axioms and postulates and may differ for different geometries. Geometric logic is the basis of vision, especially in robotic systems.

Topological logic. Topological logic is.

spatial logic and uses quite simple axioms: topological invariance (Fig. 7.1), intersection, absence of intersection. Topological logic uses topological properties of objects, the presence of which means "true", the absence of which means "false".

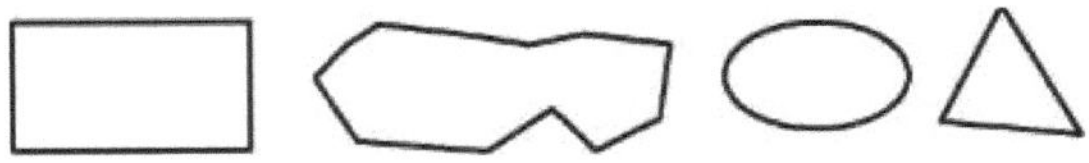

Figure 7.1. Logical correctness in topology. Topological invariants [339].

An equivalence relation exists between the figures in Fig. 7.1 there is an equivalence relation. They can be considered as logical tautologies. Fig. 7.2 shows topologically correct and topologically incorrect images. The image in Fig. 7.2a is called "spaghetti". On it, the intersections of lines are not marked and the ends of the lines extend beyond the boundaries.

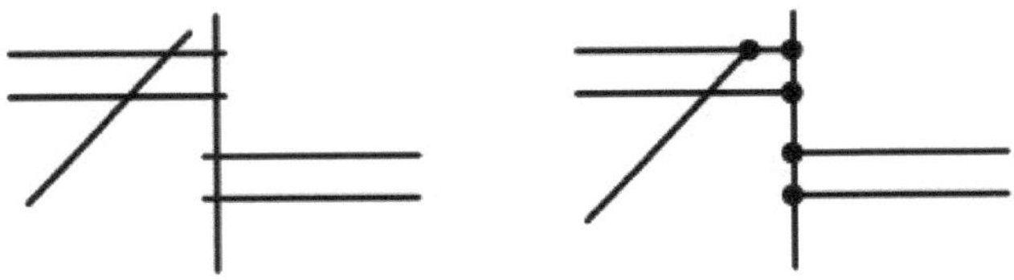

a 6

Fig.7.2 Topologically correct b) and topologically incorrect a) spatial image

The situation shown in Fig. 7.2a, occurs during automated vectorisation. It is characterised by violation of complementarity [340] and topological information correspondences. Figure 7.26 characterises the error corrections that Figure 7.2a contains. Intersections labelled by dots have been introduced, and the ends of lines extending beyond the boundaries have been trimmed. Figure 7.26 can be considered as correct from the point of view of topological logic.

In some cases topological models can be transformed into logical expressions. For example, an oriented arc corresponds to implication. Intersection corresponds to conjunction. Topological invariance corresponds to equivalence. This allows us to construct formal logical sequences corresponding to flat topologies. In topological logic, logical schemes are constructed according to topological schemes. A topological scheme represents relations.

Set-theoretic logic. Set-theoretic logic is spatial in the possibility of reflecting set-theoretic relations with the help of abstract figures. Set-theoretic logic uses set-theoretic relations as logical relations between sets. Theoretic-multiplicity diagrams display relations, unlike relations in topology. Formal expressions, or set-theoretic language, correspond to spatial relations of spatial abstract images. The most striking models are Euler-Wien diagrams.

Image logic. Figurative logic operates with spatial images that contain semantics. Figurative logic includes elementary models of objects and a priori knowledge about objects and their properties (semantics). Examples of such images are conventional signs on maps and units of spatial aggregation. Image logic is applied in geoinformatics and cartography. The most striking section of figurative logic is cartographic logic.

Cartographic logic. Cartographic logic is structurally similar to geometric logic. It is based on certain rules (axioms) and standardised information units - conventional signs. From 1908 (map logic) [341] to 2010 (cartographic logic) [342] and up to the present time, map logic is understood only as the rules of map construction and map reading, but not as the language of logic. Map logic (but not cartographic logic) is also referred to [341] as the application of ordinary logic to construct and analyse spatial cartographic images. Conversely, the notion of a language of maps has been introduced in cartography [343], but in isolation from cartographic logic. The closest to spatial logic and, accordingly, cartographic logic is the work of A. A. Lyutoy "language of maps" [343]. The peculiarity of geographical maps as spatial images and spatial models is the use of information spatial language of maps. This spatial language allows: visibility or visibility; showing with exaggeration; showing the dynamics of phenomena not directly perceived by the senses (e.g., magnetic declination, anomalies of gravity, etc.), showing spatial relations, for example, between the sources of raw materials and enterprises for its processing.

7.2. Languages of spatial logic

Bertrand Russell interpreted the nature of spatial images in this way: "There is a difficulty about language as a method of representing a system, namely that the words which signify relations are not themselves relations. The graphic image of a map is superior to language because the fact that one place is west of another is represented by the fact that the corresponding place on the map is to the left of the other, that is, the actual relation is represented by a spatial relation" [344, c. 152]. This corresponds very closely to the concepts of spatial logic, which had not yet emerged in his time.

The peculiarity of spatial languages is contradictory and ambiguous. This leads to logical errors in the construction and interpretation of cartographic images. Lyutyi distinguishes four types of errors [343]. These errors are characteristic not only for cartography, but also for all figurative logic.

The first type includes errors of *"similarity-difference"* These errors are caused by the use of graphic signs of different semiotic type, which create similar in appearance final figurative constructions. They are detected only at the level of analysing separately taken legends and maps (Fig. 7.3) [343]

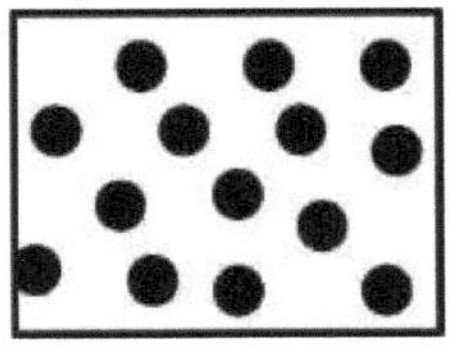

Figure 7.3. Duality of spatial image interpretation.

The spatial model in Fig. 7.3 can be interpreted in two ways. The first interpretation (I1) is that Fig. 7.3 depicts single objects. This is the individualised object interpretation. In this interpretation, each point is a separate object and these objects are densely located in a given area. This interpretation describes a set of objects in the areal.

The second interpretation (I2) of Fig. 7.3 is that it is an areal with the conventional labelling of point-filling. It is a conditional type areal whose semantic content is denoted by dots. This interpretation describes one areal, and its fill or dots show the quality of that areal. In this case, dots are conventional cartographic signs of areal type.

The second type of spatial logical errors includes errors that arise due to incorrect placement of signs in the field of cartographic image. These errors lead to the appearance of false sign compositions and relations, as well as to the effects of "absorption" of some signs by others. This group includes errors of semantic uncertainty and duplication of information (Fig. 7.4).

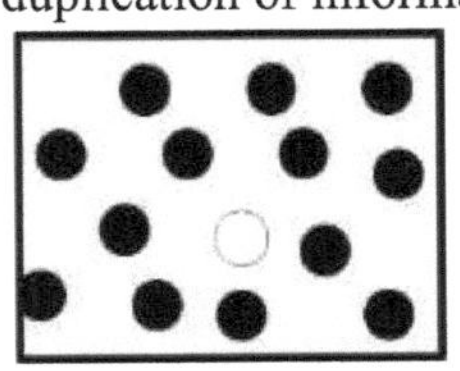

Figure 7.4: Duality of treatment on the areal

In Fig. 7.4, there is one light-coloured point object among a set of black point objects. The first interpretation (I3) of Fig. 7.4 is that it is a point-filled areal with a single object depicted by a light dot.

The second interpretation (I4) of Fig. 7.4 is that it is a point-filled areal with one point erroneously shown in white and no objects on the areal. Figure 7.5 shows the ambiguity of the objects interpretation.

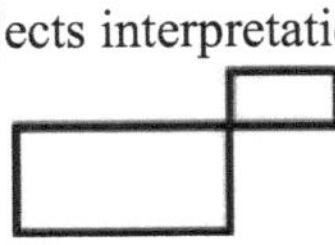

Figure 7.5: Duality of treatment of objects.

Figure 7.5 shows a fragment of a plan showing two objects. These objects are either adjacent and there is no passage between them (I5), or there is a small passage between them not visible in the scale of the plan (Ib).

To the third group A.A. Lyutyi refers errors in sign systems caused by errors in classifications of spatial objects. The fourth type includes errors in design and construction of cartographic scales. The first three types of errors are characteristic of figurative logic in general.

Another section of figurative logic is project logic. *Design logic.* This logic is used in computer-aided design (CAD) and drawing construction and in GIS for designing electronic maps. This logic is used in geographic information systems in building and editing spatial models [345]. This logic is used in analysing and acquiring spatial knowledge.

Design logic has its own languages, which are more often languages of graphical primitives, i.e. basic graphical information units from which complex information units and models of spatial objects are built (Fig. 7.6).

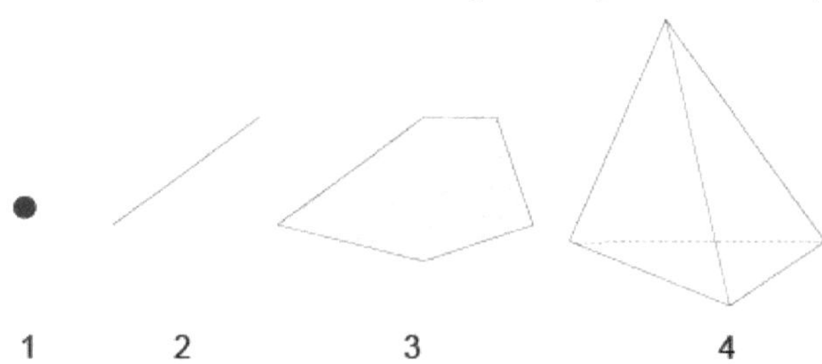

Fig. 7.6. Graphical information units - the basis for building spatial images.

When analysing spatial relations, the language of spatial aggregation is used. This language is related to spatial figurative logic. Fig. 7.7 shows logical information units expressing spatial relations between objects.

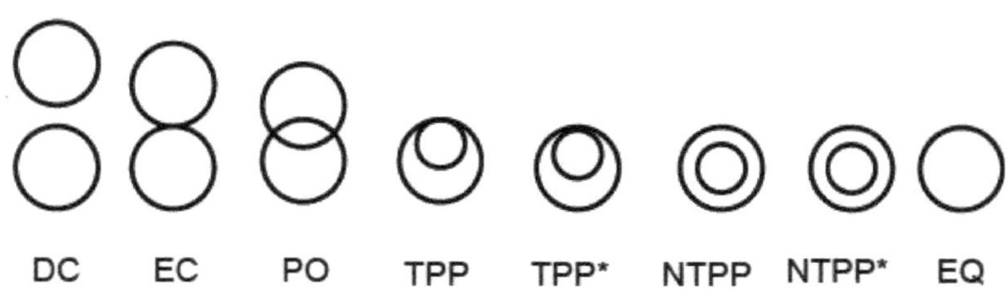

Figure 7.7. Logical units of spatial relations

Figure 7.7 describes some possible arrangements of objects relative to each other. As shown in Figure 7.4, when using only graphics, ambiguity of interpretation is possible. Therefore, in some cases, spatial logic and spatial images are supplemented with semantics that exclude ambiguity of interpretation. It should be noted. that the language of spatial aggregation is not related to the language of maps and cartography. This language is designed for abstract reasoning about possible relations between objects to model the semantics of spatial relations.

In Fig. 7.7 has the following notations adopted in the language of spatial aggregation. They are used as logical information units reflecting spatial relations of two objects. The interpretation is given from left to right. The absence of interaction is DC. Common boundary interaction - EC. Partial overlap - PO. Tangentially correct interaction TPP. Inverse tangentially correct interaction - TPP*. Object internal does not interact tangentially with object external - NTPP. An object external does not interact tangentially with an object internal - NTPP*. Objects are equivalent - EQ.

The SAL spatial aggregation language allows users to explore spatial knowledge specifications such as neighbourhood relations and equivalence predicates, and to interactively and graphically explore and modify the results. This language is one of many informatics languages. The SAL source set can be downloaded from www.cs.www.cs.purdue.edu/homes/cbk/sal.html.edu/homes/cbk/sal.html or www.parc.com/zhao/www.parc.com/zhao/sal .html.

The most common tasks in spatial logic are verification, identification, construction, and editing tasks. Pattern logic can be interpreted as any geometric properties of spatial objects or spatial relations defined in different domains: topological connectedness of domains, parallelism of lines or, equally, remoteness of two points from the third.

An important conclusion from this analysis is the need to apply information units for possible spatial analyses and logical reasoning.

7.3. Analysing the state of spatial logic.

To a large extent, the development of spatial logic has long been influenced by geometry and the geometric approach. Logical reasoning was performed in the plane in one layer using figures similar to geometric ones.

In the modern understanding, spatial logic is close to the more researched area of modal logic and temporal logic. A significant contribution to the development of spatial logic by analysing geometry and its logic was made by Tarski [346]. In particular, Tarski applied first-order logic with pointwise variables in the Euclidean plane and with non-logical predicates denoting two primitive spatial relations: the ternary relation "between" and the quaternary relation "equidistant". The resulting language is sufficient to formulate much of Euclidean geometry - for example, Pythagoras' theorem.

In Tarski's elementary geometry [24] the variables are arranged by the set of points on the Euclidean plane. This is analogous to the arrangement, in his Geometry of Solids the variables are arranged by the set of regular closed subsets of R^3 ; and in his modal topological language the variables are arranged by the set of all subsets of some topological space. Tarski showed that elementary geometry theory is decidable: there is a logical procedure for determining for any given proposition in the corresponding language whether that proposition is true according to the advertised interpretation. In contrast, the second-order theory required to express all of Hilbert's axioms is intractable.

The most distinctive feature of modern logic is the model-theoretic approach. It is vividly represented in spatial logic. The model-theoretic approach to logic often uses different relations between mathematical structures and objects as the main problem. From this point of view, spatial logic becomes a tool for studying relations between geometrical structures and real spatial objects.

The development of spatial logic was promoted by works on automation of logical inference and automation of pattern recognition. However, the more complex an image is, the more complex its processing and construction. In this context, the problem of balancing the expressive power of an image and the computational complexity of a spatial model is central to spatial logic.

Spatial logic differs from mathematical logic in three main ways. The first one concerns qualitatively different sets of geometric objects that require different logics and different interpretations: points, lines, areas of different kinds, surfaces, volumetric bodies. The second fundamental difference concerns the choice of qualitatively different basic units of description, basic relations and operations on these objects. In this difference, information units are qualitatively different. In mathematical logic they are only formal. And in spatial logic formal and semantic information units are used. The third fundamental difference concerns purely the introduction of uncertainty and modality into logical spatial descriptions. For example, the situation that object A is closer to object B than object B belongs to the field of probabilistic logic and qualitative reasoning.

The basis of transformations in mathematical logic are tautologies and equivalences. Invariance in spatial logic is a full analogue of equivalence or tautology in mathematical logic. An example is topological invariants. Many invariance relations can correspond exactly to first-order logic.

The main problem of spatial logic is the "generalisation-detail" or "simplicity-complexity" relation. The analysis of the complexity of spatial logic models usually focuses on two problems: model checking (determining whether a given model is true in the interpretation of the object corresponding to it) and checking the computational feasibility of a given model. Often an attempt to represent a spatial model in words is doomed to failure due to the limitations of linguistic tools.

Most logics above first order, contain contradictions and lead to unsolvable problems of mapping spatial images. An alternative example of decidable logics are spatial logics interpreted by regular topological models. The language of these logics includes only Boolean bundles (without quantifiers), spatial information units (primitives) and represent various topological relations and functions.

The general methodology of spatial logic analysis is to find spatial models that are logically analysable. Conventional methods of analysis that deal with simple logical models are often powerless when faced with multi-valued spatial models or structures, as is usually the case in spatial logic.

In terms of expressiveness of interpretation, the advantages and effectiveness of spatial logic should be noted. Spatial logic involves associative connections and cognitive images. This expands the possibility of interpreting a spatial image compared to its formulaic representation.

Graphical representations in spatial logic, unlike the apparatus of mathematical logic, have resources for expressing various kinds of uncertainty. The main difference between graphical and linguistic systems is the use of relations.

Spatial models use spatial relations to represent the subject area directly. In linguistic systems, words are used to represent relations indirectly and can be interpreted differently, depending on the intelligence of the interpreter.

Modern spatial logic is characterised by its wide application in science, but the absence of a unified theory. The general concept of spatial logic is the use of spatial information units. An example is cartographic conventional signs. Theoretical-multiple logic reflects spatial relations, so it can be considered as a part of spatial logic. Topological logic reflects relations. These logics complement each other when dealing with a wide set of spatial images. The higher efficiency of spatial logics is that they contain semantics and are more expressive, while mathematical logics do not contain semantics to the same extent. This ensures that the representation is expressive by means of spatial logics. The effectiveness of spatial logic is due to the possibility of expressing spatial relations by means of graphics, which increases the speed of human analysis of such models by orders of magnitude. The main problem of spatial logic, important for artificial intelligence, is the contradiction between great

expressiveness and complexity of its modelling.
A development of spatial logic are stratified or layered spatial constructions and patterns of conceptual blending [347, 348]. Conceptual blending creates
spatial images that humans are unable to imagine in advance or predict.

Literature

1. Tsvetkov V. Y., Lonskiy I. I., Bulgakov S. V. V. General and applied geoinformatics : textbook. - Moscow : MAKS Press, 2021. - 200 c/
2. Ivannikov A.D., Kulagin V.P., Tikhonov A.N., Tsvetkov V.Y. Applied Geoinformatics. - Moscow: MAKS Press, 2005. -360 c.
3. Bulgakov S. V. Applied geoinformatics : textbook. - Moscow : MAKS Press, 2019. - 72 c.
4. Borodko A.V., Bugayevskiy L.M., Vereshchaka T.V., Zapryagaeva L.A., Ivanova L.G., Knizhnikov Y.F., Savinykh V.P., Spiridonov A.I., Filatov V.N., Tsvetkov V.Ya. GEODESIA, CARTOGRAPHY, GEOINFORMATICS, CADASTR. Encyclopaedia. In 2 volumes. / Edited by A.V. Borodko, V.P. Savinykh. - Moscow, 2008. Volume I A-M.
5. Gospodinov S. G. New view on geoinformatics // Vector GeoSciences. G. A new look at geoinformatics // Vector GeoSciences. 2022. T. 5. № 3. C. 80-89.
6. Buravtsev A. V. Geoinformatics science of space// Slavic Forum. -2020. - 4(30). -c.161-170
7. Maksudova L.G., Savinykh V.P., Tsvetkov V.Ya. Integration of sciences about the surrounding world in geoinformatics // Earth Exploration from Space. - 2000. - №1. - c.46-50.
8. Maksudova L.G., Savinykh V.P., Tsvetkov V.Ya. About interdisciplinary integration on the basis of geoinformatics// Izvestiya vysshee obrazovaniye vysshee obrazovaniye. Geodesy and aerial photography. - 2004. - № 5. - c.110-117.
9. Matchin, V.T. Integrated geoinformation space // Slavic Forum. -2018. - 3(21). - c.21-27.
10. Polyakov A.A., Tsvetkov V.Y. Applied Informatics. - M.: Janus-K, 2002. - 392 c.
11. Tsvetkov V.Ya. Geoinformation systems and technologies - M.: Finance and Statistics, 1998. -288 c.
12. Ivannikov A.D., Kulagin V.P., Tikhonov A.N., Tsvetkov V.Y. Geoinformatics. - Moscow: MAKS Press, 2001. -349c
13. Tsvetkov V.Ya. Geoinformatics and overcoming information barriers // Izvestiya vysshee obrazovaniya vysshee obrazovaniya. Geodesy and aerial photography. - 2004. - №6. - c.113-118
14. Savinykh V.P., Tsvetkov V.Ya. Geoinformatics as a tool for studying the processes of globalisation // Earth Sciences. - 2011. - №003-04. - c.3138.
15. Butko E. Я. Geoinformatics as a method of building a picture of the world // Slavic Forum. - 2017. - №. 1. - C. 34-41.

16. Koshkarev A.. V. Geoinformatics in the infrastructural support of the digital economy // Geodesy and Cartography. - 2019. - T. 80. - №. 1. - C. 119-126.
17. Xiao W. et al. Geoinformatics for the conservation and promotion of cultural heritage in support of the UN Sustainable Development Goals //ISPRS Journal of Photogrammetry and Remote Sensing. - 2018. - T. 142. - C. 389-406..
18. Gvishiani A. D. et al. Geoinformatics and systems analysis in geophysics and geodynamics //Izvestiya, Physics of the Solid Earth. - 2019. - T. 55. - №. 1. - C. 33-49.
19. Karimi H. A. (ed.). Big Data: techniques and technologies in geoinformatics. - Crc Press, 2014.
20. Awange J. L. et al. Algebraic geodesy and geoinformatics. - Springer Science & Business Media, 2010.
21. Monakhov C.B., Savinykh V.P., Tsvetkov V.Y. General geoinformatics. - M.: Max Press 2004 - 100 pp.
22. Kudzh S.A., Tsvetkov V.Y. Geoinformatics: Monograph. - Moscow: MAKS Press, 2019. - 224 c.
23. Tsvetkov V. Ya. Fundamentals of geoinformatics: textbook for EE. - St. Petersburg: Lan, 2020. - 188 c.
24. Tsvetkov V. *Ya*. Fundamentals of geoinformatics: textbook for EE. - St. Petersburg: Lan, 2023. - 186 c.
25. Savinykh V.P., Tsvetkov V.Ya. Development of artificial intelligence methods in geoinformatics // Transport of the Russian Federation. - 2010. - № 5. - c.41-43.
26. Buchkin D.V. State and development of intellectual GIS // Information and Space. 2020. - №3. -c .119-123.
27. Shaitura S. V. Information resources in geoinformatics // Educational resources and technologies. - 2015. - №1(9). - c.103-108.
28. Tsvetkov V.Y., Rosenberg I.N. Intelligent transport systems - Saarbrucken, 2012. - 297 c.
29. Mayorov A.A., Tsvetkov V.Ya. Geoinformatics as the most important direction of informatics development // Information Technologies. - 2013. - № 11. - c.2-7.
30. Chandrasekar K. Informatics: An Emerging Discipline of the Information Age //Jaffna Science Ass. - 2013. - T. 19. - №. 2. - C. 4.
31. Bauer F., Gooz G. Informatics. - M.: Mir, 1976. - 486 c.
32. Savinykh V.P., Tsvetkov V.Ya. Integration of GIS technologies and Earth remote sensing systems // Earth Exploration from Space. - 2000. - №2. -

c.83-86.
33. Vanicek P., Krakiwsky E. J. Geodesy: the concepts. - Elsevier Science Publisher B.V. 1986 reprinted by Elsevier, 2015. - 778p. ISBN 0444-87775-4.
34. Tsvetkov V.Ya. Spatial relations in geoinformatics// Earth Sciences. - 2012. - №1. - c.59-61
35. Tsvetkov V.Ya. Types of spatial relations // Uspekhi sovremennoi naukhnostvosnaniya. - 2013. - № 5 - c.138-140.
36. Tsvetkov V.Ya. On spatial and economic relations // International Journal of Experimental Education. - 2013. - №3. - c.115-117.
37. Bakhareva N.A. Analysis of spatial relations // Slavic Forum. 2021, 3(33). C.7-15
38. Tsvetkov V.Ya. Spatial knowledge // International Journal of Applied and Fundamental Research. - 2013. - №7. - c.43-47.
39. Kuzhelev P. D. Spatial knowledge for transport management // State Counsellor. - 2016. - №2. - c 17-22.
40. Munzer S., Lorch L., Frankenstein J. Wayfinding and acquisition of spatial knowledge with navigation assistance //Journal of Experimental Psychology: Applied. - 2020. - T. 26. - №. 1. - C. 73
41. Tsvetkov V.Ya. Formation of spatial knowledge: Monograph. - Moscow: MAKS Press, 2015. - 68 c.
42. Maksimova M.V. Coordinate support of geodetic monitoring // Earth Sciences" № 1-2013 - p.49-54.
43. Rosenberg I.N., Tsvetkov V.Y. Coordinate systems in geoinformatics - MGUPS, 2009. -67 c
44. Tsvetkov V.Ya. Coordinate systems in geoinformatics. - M.: Max Press 2005 - 49 p.
45. Yip, K., and Zhao, F. Spatial aggregation: theory and applications. // 1996. Journal of Artificial Intelligence Research, 5,1-26.
46. Glushkov V. V., Nasretdinov K. K., Sharavin A.. A. Space geodesy: methods and prospects of development. - Institute for Political and Military Analysis, 2002.- 448 pp.
47. Oznamets V.V. The Evolution of Space Geodesy // Russian Journal of Astrophysical Research. Series A, 2023,9(1). C. 14-19.
48. Oznamets V.V., Tsvetkov V.Ya. Space geodesy of small celestial bodies // Russian Journal of Astrophysical Research. Series A. 2019, 5(1). c. 30-40
49. Gospodinov S. G. The Development of Geodesic Astronomy // Russian Journal of Astrophysical Research. Series A, 2018, 4(1). C. 9-33

50. Gospodinov S.G. Evolution of geodetic astronomy // Russian Journal of
Astrophysical Research. Series A, 2022,8(1). C. 3-11.
51. Plakhov Y.V. Krasnorylov I.I. Geodesic astronomy. - M.: Kartocentre-Geodesizdat, 2002. -390c.
52. Gospodinov G.S. Geodesic astronomy and space geoinformatics // Railways Science and Technology. - 2017. - 1(1). - c.45-50/
53. Kaula W. M. Theory of satellite geodesy: applications of satellites to geodesy. - Courier Corporation, 2013.
54. Savinykh V.P. Development of space geoinformatics // Slavic forum, 2016. -2(12). - c.223-230.
55. V. G. Bondur, V. Ya. Tsvetkov. New Scientific Direction of Space Geoinformatics // European Journal of Technology and Design, 2015, 4 (10), pp. 118-126.
56. Savinykh V.P. New view on geodesy // ITNOU:
Information technology in science, education and management. - 2019. - № 1. - c. 58-63.
57. Gudehus G., Touplikiotis A. On the stability of geotechnical systems and its fractal progressive loss //Acta Geotechnica. - 2018. - T. 13. - №. 2. - C. 317328.
58. Tsvetkov, V.Ya.; Kuzhelev, P.D. Railway as a geotechnical system // Uspekhi sovremennoi nauchnostvosnaniya. -2009. - №4. - c. 52/
59. Bakhareva N.A. Geotechnical systems // Slavic Forum. 2023, 2(40). C. 27-37.
60. Big Soviet Encyclopaedia: In 30 vol. - Moscow: "Soviet Encyclopaedia", 1969-1978/.
61. Raymond A. J. et al. Review of impact categories and environmental indicators for life cycle assessment of geotechnical systems // Journal of Industrial Ecology. - 2020. - T. 24. - №. 3. - C. 485-499.
62. Chowdhury R. N., Xu D. W. Geotechnical system reliability of slopes //Reliability Engineering & System Safety. - 1995. - T. 47. - №. 3. - C. 141-151.
63. Zhang J., Zhang L. M., Tang W. H. Reliability-based optimisation of geotechnical systems //Journal of Geotechnical and Geoenvironmental Engineering. H. Reliability-based optimisation of geotechnical systems // Journal of Geotechnical and Geoenvironmental Engineering. - 2011. - T. 137. - №. 12. - C. 1211-1221.
64. Zhang J., Zhang L. M., Tang W. H. Reliability-based optimisation of geotechnical systems //Journal of Geotechnical and Geoenvironmental

Engineering. H. Reliability-based optimisation of geotechnical systems // Journal of Geotechnical and Geoenvironmental Engineering. - 2011. - T. 137. - №. 12. - C. 1211-1221.
65. Li D. Q. et al. Bivariate distribution of shear strength parameters using copulas and its impact on geotechnical system reliability //Computers and Geotechnics. - 2015. - T. 68. - C. 184-195
66. Elmekati A., El Shamy U. A practical co-simulation approach for multiscale analysis of geotechnical systems //Computers and Geotechnics. - 2010. - T. 37. - №. 4. - C. 494-503
67. Basu D., Misra A., Puppala A. J. Sustainability and geotechnical engineering: perspectives and review //Canadian geotechnical journal. - 2015. - T. 52. - №. 1. - C. 96-113.
68. Zhang W. et al. Application of deep learning algorithms in geotechnical engineering: a short critical review //Artificial Intelligence Review. - 2021. - C. 1-41
69. Wood D. M. Geotechnical modelling. - CRC press, 2003. - T. 1.
70. Phoon K. K., Tang C. Characterisation of geotechnical model uncertainty //Georisk: Assessment and Management of Risk for Engineered Systems and Geohazards. - 2019. - T. 13. - №. 2. - C. 101-130.
71. Raymond A. J. et al. Review of impact categories and environmental indicators for life cycle assessment of geotechnical systems // Journal of Industrial Ecology. - 2020. - T. 24. - №. 3. - C. 485-499.
72. Abaturova I. et al. Ensuring the sustainable functioning of the geotechnical system of mineral deposits in difficult engineering and geological conditions //25th European Meeting of Environmental and Engineering Geophysics. - EAGE Publications BV, 2019. - T. 2019. - №. 1. - C. 1-5.
73. Rosenberg I.N., Voznesenskaya M.E. Geocognition and georeference.// Bulletin of Moscow State Regional Pedagogical University. - 2010. - № 2. - c. 116-118.
74. Tsvetkov V. Ya. Geoknowledge // European Journal of Technology and Design. - 2016, 3(13), pp. 122-132.
75. Baghbani A. et al. Application of artificial intelligence in geotechnical engineering: A state-of-the-art review //Earth-Science Reviews. - 2022. - T. 228. - C.103991
76. Klyuev P. V. et al. Complex analysis of the application of effective technologies to improve the sustainable development of the natural-technical system // Sustainable development of mountain territories. - 2020. - T. 12. - №. 2. - C. 283-290.
77. Suzdaleva A. L. Creation of controlled natural-technical systems //

Natural and Technical Sciences. - 2016. - №. 8. - C. 43-46.
78. Maslikov V. I., Fedorov M. P. Natural-technical systems in power engineering // Izvestia of the Russian Academy of Sciences. Energetics. - 2006. - №. 5. - C. 7-16.
79. DeJong J., Tibbett M., Fourie A. Geotechnical systems that evolve with ecological processes //Environmental earth sciences. - 2015. - T. 73. - C. 10671082.
80. Tsvetkov V.Ya. Theory of systems. - M.: MAKS Press, 2018. - 88 c.
81. Nomokonova O.Yu Complex data systems // Slavic Forum. - 2019. - 2(24). - c.129-136
82. Pavlov, A.I. Complex organisational systems // Slavic Forum. -2018. - 4 (22). - c.54-59
83. Buravtsev, A.V. Complex technological systems// Slavic Forum. - 2017. -4(18). - c.14-19.
84. Tsvetkov V. Ya. Informatisation: Creation of modern information technologies. Part 1. Data structures and technical means. - Moscow: SCST, VSTCentre, 1990. - 118 c.
85. Tsvetkov V.Ya. Complex technical systems // Educational resources and technologies - 2017.-3 (20). - c.86-92
86. Rosenberg I.N., Soloviev I.V., Tsvetkov V.Ya. Complex innovations in the management of complex organisational and technical systems. / edited by V.I. Yakunin - M.: Feoria, 2010. - 248 c.
87. Tsvetkov V.Ya. Relation, connection, correspondence // Slavic Forum, 2016. -2(12). - c.272-276.
88. Tsvetkov V.Ya. Application of geoinformation technologies for decision-making support // Izvestiya vysokikh uchebnykh obrazovaniya. Geodesy and aerial photography. - 2001. - №4. - c.128-138.
89. Bulgakov S.V., Kovalchuk A.V., Tsvetkov V.Y., Shaitura S.V. Integrated geoinformation systems. - Moscow: Bauman Moscow State Technical University, 2007 - 113 p.
90. Tsvetkov, V.Ya. Geoinformation geotechnical monitoring // Earth Sciences. - 2012.-№4. c.054-058.
91. Bulgakov, S.V. Geotechnical monitoring of transport // Science and technology of railways. 2021. T. 5. №1 (17). - c.42-49
92. Markelov V.M., Tsvetkov V.Y. Geomonitoring// Slavic Forum, 2015. -2(8). - c.177-184
93. Elsukov P. Yu. Development of geomonitoring// Slavic Forum. - 2020. - 4(30). -c.55-65.
94. Tsvetkov V.Ya. Applied systems // Izvestia vysshee obrazovaniya

vysshee obrazovaniya. Geodesy and aerial photography. - 2005. - №3. - c.76-85.
95. Tsvetkov V.Ya. Geoinformation monitoring // Izvestiya vysshee obrazovaniya vysshee obrazovaniya. Geodesy and aerial photography. - 2005. - №5. - c.151 -155.
96. Rosenberg I.N., Tsvetkov V.Ya. Semiotic management of transport systems // Slavic Forum, 2015. - 2(8) - c.275-282
97. Tsvetkov, V.Ya. Semiotic approach to the construction of data models in automated information systems // Izvestiya vysokikh uchebnykh obrazovaniya. Geodesy and aerial photography. - 2000. - №5. - c. 142-145
98. Tsvetkov V.Ya. Paralinguistic information units in education// Perspectives of Science and Education. - 2013. - 4(4). - c.30-38
99. Kuj A. S. Geodata collection and measurement in Earth Sciences// Slavic Forum. - 2013. - 2(4). - c.135-139
100. Matchin V.T. Formation of geodata// Slavic Forum, 2015. - 2(8) - c.185-193.
101. Tsvetkov V.Ya., Shaitura S.V., Minitaeva A.M., Feoktistova V.M., Kozhaev Yu.P., Belyu L.P. Metamodelling in the information field // Amazonia Investiga. 2020. T. 9. № 25. C. 395-402.
102. Buravtsev A.B., Tsvetkov V.Ya. Cloud computing for big geospatial data // Information and Space. 2019. - №3. -c .110115.
103. Levin B.A., Tsvetkov V.Ya. Information processes in the space of "big data" // World of Transport. 2017. - T.15, №6(73). - c.20-30.
104. Tsvetkov, V.Ya., Oznamets, V.V.. Big data in geodetic support // Geodesy and Cartography. 2022. T. 83. № 10. C. 9-19.
105. Hancock J. T., Khoshgoftaar T. M. CatBoost for big data: an interdisciplinary review // Journal of big data. - 2020. - T. 7. - №. 1. - C. 1-45.
106. Deepa N. et al. A survey on blockchain for big data: Approaches, opportunities, and future directions //Future Generation Computer Systems. - 2022. - T. 131. - C. 209-226.
107. Wang J. et al. Big data service architecture: a survey // Journal of Internet Technology. - 2020. - T. 21. - №. 2. - C. 393-405.
108. Baghbani A. et al. Application of artificial intelligence in geotechnical engineering: A state-of-the-art review //Earth-Science Reviews. - 2022. - T. 228.
- C. 103991
109. Mitchell J. K., Santamarina J. C. Biological considerations in geotechnical engineering //Journal of geotechnical and geoenvironmental engineering. - 2005. - T. 131. - №. 10. - C. 1222-1233

110. Tsvetkov V. Ya. Geotechnical system // Actual issues of modern science and education. - 2021. - C. 144-151.
111. Udachin V. N. N., Aminov P. G., Williamson B. D. Geochemistry of the environment of geotechnical systems of the Southern Urals // Natural and Technical Sciences. D. Environmental geochemistry of geotechnical systems of the Southern Urals // Natural and Technical Sciences. - 2009. - №. 6. - C. 298-306.
112. Carri A. et al. Advantages of IoT-based geotechnical monitoring systems integrating automatic procedures for data acquisition and elaboration //Sensors. - 2021. - T. 21. - №. 6. - C. 2249.
113. Tsang H. H., Pitilakis K. Mechanism of geotechnical seismic isolation system: Analytical modelling //Soil Dynamics and Earthquake Engineering. - 2019. - T. 122. - C. 171-184.
114. Barrile V. et al. Integration of geomatics methodologies and creation of a cultural heritage app using augmented reality //Virtual Archaeology Review. - 2019. - T. 10. - №. 20. - C. 40-51.
115. Barrile V., Fotia A., Bilotta G. Geomatics and augmented reality experiments for the cultural heritage //Applied Geomatics. - 2018. - T. 10. - №. 4. - C. 569-578.
116. El-Zeiny A. M., El Kafrawy S. B., Ahmed M. H. Geomatics based approach for assessing Qaroun Lake pollution //The Egyptian Journal of Remote Sensing and Space Science. - 2019. - T. 22. - №. 3. - C. 279-296.
117. Ogundare J. O. Understanding least squares estimation and geomatics data analysis. - John Wiley & Sons, 2018.
118. ISO OSI/TC 211: Geographic Information/ Geomatics, International Draft Standard.
119. Golubev B.B., Fartukova I.S., Tsvetkov V.Y. International Conference "Education in the field of geodesy, cadastre and land management: trends of globalisation and convergence" // Geodesy and Cartography - 2012.- № 10. - c56-59
120. Tsvetkov V.Ya. International Conference "Education in the field of geodesy, cadastre and land management: trends of globalisation and convergence"// Engineering Surveys. -2012. - № 11. - c.12-14
121. Tsvetkov V.Ya. Creation of integrated information basis of GIS// Izvestiya vysshee obrazovaniya vysshee obrazovaniya. Geodesy and aerial photography. - 2000. - №4. - c.150-154.
122. Rosenberg I.N. Geoinformation model // International Journal of Applied and Fundamental Research. - 2016. - №5-4. - c. 675-676
123. Ozherelieva T.A. Information situation as a management tool // Slavic

Forum, 2016. -4(14). - c.176-181.
124. Tsvetkov V.Ya. Systematics of information situations // Perspectives of Science and Education. - 2016. - №5 (23). - c.64-68.
125. Pavlov A.I. Spatial information situation // Slavic Forum, 2016. - 4(14). - c.198-203.
126. Tsvetkov V. Ya. Situational modelling in geoinformatics // Information technologies. - 2014. - №6. - c.64-69
127. ISO/TR 19122:2004(en) Geographic information/Geomatics - Qualification and certification of personnel.
128. ACSG - Association canadienne des sciences geomatiques (Section Champlain) /// Des references utiles en geomatique". acsg-champlain.scg.ulaval.ca.
129. Arrete du 27 decembre 1994 relatif a la terminologie de la teledetection aerospatiale, retrieved 2019-11-04.
130. Paradis, Michel (September 1981). "De l'arpentage a la geomatique". Le Geometre Canadien (in French). 35 (3): 262
131. Lexikon der Kartographie und Geomatik: in zwei Banden.- Heidelberg; Spekrum Akademisher verlag - Berlin / Bd1/ A bis Karti/ - 2001 - 453 s
132. Boehm, Richard G.; Mohan, Audrey (2010). "Geospatial Technology: Curricular Keystone of Applied Geography". International Journal of Applied Geospatial Research. 1 (1): 26-39. doi:10.4018/jagr.2010071602. ISSN 19479654.
133. Scholten, H.J.; Velde, R.; van Manen, N. (2009). Geospatial Technology and the Role of Location in Science. GeoJournal Library. Springer Netherlands. p. 1. ISBN 978-90-481-2620-0. Retrieved 2022-01-28
134. "Curtin University - Spatial science courses". Archived from the original on 2015-09-10. Retrieved 2016-07-31.
135. University of Tasmania, Centre for Spatial Information Science, Courses Archived 2008-07-25 at the Wayback Machine
136. "University of Adelaide, Major in Ecology and Spatial Science" (PDF). adelaide.edu.au. Archived from the original (PDF) on 21 August 2014. Retrieved 2 April 2018.
137. Melbourne University - Spatial Information Science[permanent dead link]
138. "Surveying and geospatial sciences - RMIT University".
139. Geospatial Engineer Jobs (12Y)". goarmy.com. Retrieved 2 April 2018.
140. 12Y Geospatial Engineer - National Guard."

www.nationalguard.com. Retrieved 2 April 2022.
141. V. Ya. Tsvetkov. Spatial Relations Economy // European Journal of Economic Studies 2013, Vol.(3), No. 1 p.57-60/
142. Romanov I.A. The state of spatial economy // Slavic Forum. - 2013. - 1(3). - c.110-115.
143. Markelov V.M. Logistics and spatial economy // Slavic Forum. - 2013. - 1(3). - pp.91-95yu
144. Tsvetkov V. Y., Bulgakov S. V. V. Logistic geoinformatics - Moscow: MAKS Press, 2023. - 192 c.
145. Todorova A.I. Application of geoinformatics in geoecology // Slavic Forum. 2023, 1(39). C. 358-362.
146. Deshko, I.P.; Tsvetkov, V.Ya. Information modelling in ecological studies of landscape // Slavic Forum. -2020. - 3(29). -c.31-43.
147. Koliopoulos T. K., Katsoni V. The innovative geoinformatics public health utilities for sustainable ecological tourism facilities //Cultural and Tourism Innovation in the Digital Era: Sixth International IACuDiT Conference, Athens 2019. - Springer International Publishing, 2020. - C. 649-659.
148. Ikonnikov V. F., Sedun A. M., Tokarevskaya N. G. Economic geoinformatics: a training programme for undergraduates. - BSEU, Minsk, 2012.-8c
149. Levin B.A., Kruglov V.M., Matveev S.I., Kougia V.A., Tsvetkov V.Ya. Geoinformatics of transport // International Journal of Experimental Education. - 2015. - № 3 - C. 223-223.
150. Levin B.A., Kruglov V.M., Matveev S.I., Tsvetkov V.Y., Kougia V.A. Geoinformatics of transport. - M.: VINITI RAN, 2006. - 336 c.
151. Bulgakov S. V. Geoinformatics of transport in the conditions of digital transformation // Science and Technology of Railways. - 2021. - T. 5. - №. 3. - C. 28-37.
152. Shaitura S.V., Kozhaev Yu. P. Geoinformatics of road transport // Slavic Forum. - 2019. - №. 3. - C. 379-386.
153. Tsvetkov V.Y., Savinykh V.P. Space geoinformatics: textbook for universities. - St. Petersburg: Lan, 2022. - 184 c.
154. Rajakaruna N., Boyd S. Geoecology //Oxford Bibliographies in Ecology. - 2014.
155. Nyrtsov M. V. Development of theory and methodology of mapping of small celestial bodies. Dne. on competition of academic degree of Doctor of Technical Sciences Speciality 25.00.33
- Cartography. - Moscow: MIIGAiK, 2012, - Vol.1. - 447p/.

156. Savinykh V. P., Tsvetkov V. Ya. Geoinformatics as a system of sciences // Geodesy and Cartography. - 2013. - №4. - c.52-57
157. Tebekin A. V. Logistics. - Moscow. Dashkov & K, 2018. -356c.
158. Nerush Y. M., Nerush A. Yu. Logistics. - Moscow: Yurait, 2019. - 559c.
159. Ivut, R. B. Logistics: textbook for students. - Minsk : BITU, 2021. - 462 c
160. Tien N. H., Anh D. B. H., Thuc T. D. Global supply chain and logistics management //Dehli: Academic Publications. - 2019.
161. Harrison A. et al. Logistics management and strategy: competing through the supply chain. - Pearson UK, 2019.
162. Raev V.K., Tsvetkov V.Ya. Logical chains // Distance and virtual learning. 2018. - № 1(120). - c.14-21
163. Winarno H. et al. Food hubs and short food supply chain, efforts to realise regional food distribution centre //International Journal of Supply Chain Management. - 2020. - T. 9. - №. 3. - C. 338-350.
164. Kalaiarasan R. et al. Supply chain visibility for improving inbound logistics: a design science approach //International Journal of Production Research. - 2022. - C. 1-16.
165. Nogueira G. P. M. et al. The environmental impact of fast delivery B2C e-commerce in outbound logistics operations: A simulation approach //Cleaner Logistics and Supply Chain. - 2022. - T. 5. - C. 100070.
166. Haralambides H. E. Gigantism in container shipping, ports and global logistics: a time-lapse into the future //Maritime Economics & Logistics. - 2019. - T. 21. - №. 1. - C. 1-60.
167. Selviaridis K., Norrman A. Performance-based contracting for advanced logistics services: challenges in its adoption, design and management //International Journal of Physical Distribution & Logistics Management. - 2015.
168. Uusitalo J. A framework for CTL method-based wood procurement logistics //International Journal of Forest Engineering. - 2005. - T. 16. - №. 2. - C. 37-46.
169. Tsvetkov V.Ya., Oznamets B.B., Filatov B.H. Solution of the Launhardt problem in a fuzzy situation. // Information and Space. -2018. - №4. - c. 103-109
170. Konstantakopoulos G. D., Gayialis S. P., Kechagias E. P. Vehicle routing problem and related algorithms for logistics distribution: A literature review and classification //Operational research. - 2022. - T. 22. - №. 3. - C. 2033-2062.

171. Xu J., Shi Y., Zhao S. Reverse logistics network-based multiperiod optimisation for construction and demolition waste disposal //Journal of Construction Engineering and Management. - 2019. - T. 145. - №. 2. - C. 04018124.
172. Prajapati H., Kant R., Shankar R. Bequeath life to death: state-of-the-art review on reverse logistics //Journal of cleaner production. - 2019. - T. 211. - C. 503-520.
173. Baah C., Jin Z., Tang L. Organisational and regulatory stakeholder pressures friends or foes to green logistics practices and financial performance: investigating corporate reputation as a missing link // Journal of cleaner production. - 2020. - T. 247. - C. 119125.
174. Russell S. H. Growing world of logistics //Air Force Journal of Logistics. - 2000. - T. 24. - №. 4. - C. 12.
175. Wegelius-Lehtonen T. Performance measurement in construction logistics //International journal of production economics. - 2001. - T. 69. - №. 1. - C. 107-116.
176. Troll K. Landscape ecology (geoecology) and biogeocenology, terminological study // Izvestia AS USSR. Ser.
Geographical. 1972. №3. C. 114-120.
177. Fogel M. L. 14. Geoecology //Geochemical Perspectives. - 2019. - T. 8. - №. 2. - C. 219-229.
178. Broothaerts N. et al. Changes in floodplain geo-ecology in the Belgian loess belt during the first millennium AD //Netherlands Journal of Geosciences. - 2021. - T. 100. - C. e14.
179. Perez F. L. Geoecology of a granite dome: Spatial interactions between gnammas, rills, soils, and plant cover, Enchanted Rock (Texas, USA) //CATENA. - 2023. - T. 223. - C. 106938.
180. Oznamets V.V. Spatial modelling. - Saarbruken, 2021. -117 c.
181. Tsvetkov V.Ya. Information model as a basis for information processing in GIS // Izvestiya vysokikh uchebnykh obrazovaniye. Geodesy and aerial photography. -2005. - №2. - c.118-122.
182. Chekharin E.E. Algorithms of interpretation of remote sensing data. // Slavic Forum, 2015. - 3(9) - c.301-308.
183. Raev V.K. Information units in the information field // Slavic Forum. 2022, 1(35). C. 104-114
184. Tsvetkov V.Ya. Information models and information resources // Izvestiya vysshee obrazovaniya vysshee obrazovaniya [Izvestia of higher educational institutions]. Geodesy and aerial photography. - 2005. - №3. - c.85-91.

185. Matchin V.T. Information resources as a tool of scientific research and development // Vestnik MIREA. - 2014 - № 2 (3) - c.235-256.
186. Tsvetkov V.Ya. Designing data structures and databases - M.: Moscow State University of Geodesy and Cartography, 1997. - 90 c .
187. Matchin V.T. Updating databases with spatial information // Slavic Forum, 2015. - 3(9) - c.173-180
188. Matchin V. T. Standardisation in the creation of geodatabases // Slavic Forum, 2015. - 4(10) - c.209-216.
189. Anjo A. M. et al. Lisbon as a literary tourism site: Essays of a digital map of Pessoa as a new trigger //Journal of Tourism, Heritage & Services Marketing (JTHSM). - 2021. - T. 7. - №. 2. - C. 58-67.
190. Wadoux A. M. J. C., Minasny B., McBratney A. B. Machine learning for digital soil mapping: Applications, challenges and suggested solutions //Earth- Science Reviews. - 2020. - T. 210. - C. 103359.
191. Tsvetkov V.Ya. Digital maps and digital models // Izvestiya vysshee obrazovaniye vysshee obrazovaniye. Geodesy and aerial photography. - 2000. - №2. - c.147-155.
192. Gura D. A. et al. About prospects for the air laser scanning technology implementation for obtaining a digital model of densely built-in territories //IOP Conference Series: Materials Science and Engineering. - IOP Publishing, 2019. - T. 698. - №. 4. - C. 044014.
193. Chen Y., Matsubara T., Yaguchi T. Neural symplectic form: learning Hamiltonian equations on general coordinate systems //Advances in Neural Information Processing Systems. - 2021. - T. 34. - C. 16659-16670./
194. Kolz C. W. et al. Reliable interpretation of scapular kinematics depends on coordinate system definition //Gait & posture. - 2020. - T. 81. - C. 183-190.
195. Rodrigue J. P., Ducruet C. 2.1-the geography of transport networks. - 2020.
196. Shaw J., Hesse M. Transport, geography and the'new'mobilities //Transactions of the Institute of British Geographers. - 2010. - T. 35. - №. 3. - C. 305-312.
197. Bondur V. G., Tsvetkov V. Ya. System Analysis in Space Research // Russian Journal of Astrophysical Research. Series A. 2015. 1 (1), p. 4-12.
198. Tsvetkov V.Ya. System analysis of GIS // Educational resources and technologies. - 2015. - №1(9). - c.97-103.
199. Tsvetkov V.Y. Dichotomous systemic analysis // Life Science Journal. 2014. T. 11. № 7s. C. 246-250
200. Kudzh, S.A.; Tsvetkov, V.Ya. Modelling of the dynamic surfaces (in

Russian) // Information and Space. 2023. - №3. -c .80-85/
201. Rozenberg I.N., Tsvetkov V.Y. Transport infrastructure facilities design // In Proceedings: AIP Conference Proceedings. 2. Сер. "Proceedings of the II International Conference on Advances in Materials, Systems and Technologies, CAMSTech-II 2021" 2022. С. 060005.
202. Tsvetkov V.Ya. Qualitative analysis relations // In Proceedings: IOP Conference Series: Materials Science and Engineering. Krasnoyarsk Science and Technology City Hall., Krasnoyarsk, Russian Federation, 2021. С. 12127/
203. Tsvetkov V.Ya., Tyagunov A.M. Informational synergetics // In Proceedings: AIP Conference Proceedings. Melville, New York, United States of America, 2021. С. 50051.
204. Savinykh V.P., Tsvetkov V.Ya. Synergetic aspect of geoinformatics and remote sensing technologies// Earth Exploration from Space.- 2002.- № 5.- p.71-78.
205. Kudj S.A. Synergetics of spatial information // Perspectives of Science and Education-2014. - №5. - c.14-20.
206. Tsvetkov V.Ya. Synergetics of the information field: a monograph. - Moscow: MAKS Press, 2022. - 72 c.
207. Maksudova L.G., Tsvetkov V.Ya. Information modelling as a fundamental method of cognition // Izvestiya vysshee obrazovaniya vysshee obrazovaniya. Geodesy and aerial photography. - 2001. - №1. - c.102-106.
208. Ozherel'eva T.A. GIS as management systems // Slavic Forum. 2022, 3(37). С. 434-443.
209. Markelov V.M. GIS as transport management systems. // Izvestiya vysshee obrazovaniya vysshee obrazovaniya. Geodesy and aerial photography. 2013. - №2. - c.85. -87.
210. Tikhonov A.N., Tsvetkov V.Ya. Methods and Systems of Decision Support. - Moscow: MAKS Press, 2001. -312 c.
211. Markelov, V.M. Spatial information as a factor of management // State Counsellor. - 2013. - №4. - c34-38.
212. Ozherel'eva T.A. Spatial situational modelling // Slavic Forum. 2022, 2(36). С. 134-142.
213. Tsvetkov V.Ya. Information Management. - Saarbrucken, 2012. - 201c
214. Ozherelieva T. A. Digital Management // Slavic Forum. - 2020. - 3(29). -c.44-55.
215. Istomin E. P. et al. P. et al. Geoinformation management as a modern approach to the management of spatially-distributed systems and territories //International Multidisciplinary Scientific GeoConference Surveying

Geology and Mining Ecology Management, SGEM, Bulgaria. - 2015. - T. 1. - №. 2. - C. 607-614.
216. Cassettari S. (ed.). Introduction to integrated geo-information management. - Springer Science & Business Media, 2012.
217. Ning Z. Spatio-temporal cadastral data model: Geo-information management perspective in China. - ITC, 2006.
218. Tsvetkov V. Ya. Corporate governance // Modern Management Technologies. 2022. 4(100)
219. Ozherel'eva T.A. Informational corporate governance // Slavic Forum. 2023, 4(42). C. 90-103.
220. Tsvetkov V.Ya. Corporate governance: monograph. - Sofia. UASG. 2023. - 123 c. ISBN 978-619-7731-89-7
221. Markelov V.M. Integration of methods of geoinformatics and logistics. // Bulletin of MSTU MIREA. - 2014 - № 4 (5) - c.139-171.
222. Markelov V.M. Logistics and spatial economy // Slavic Forum. - 2013. - 1(3). - c.91-95.
223. Ozherelieva T.A. Hard and "soft" management// Slavic Forum. - 2018. - 1(19). - c.56-62
224. Oznamets V. V. Soft situational management // Slavic Forum. -2018. - 2(20). - c.57-62
225. Andreeva O.A., Tsvetkov V.Y., Oznamets V.V. Geoinformation mass modelling // Information and Space. 2020. - №2. -c .106-112
226. Oznamets V.V. Exponential and hyperbolic model of real estate valuation // Slavic Forum. -2019. - 1(23). - c.26-31
227. Gospodinov S.G. Geoinformational management of real estate. - Saarbruken, 2023. -141 c.
228. Oznamets V. V. Problems of sustainable development of territories // State Counsellor. - 2018. - №2. - c.11-19.
229. Oznamets V. V. Information support of land use // State Counsellor. - 2018. - №4(24). - c.13-19.
230. Zhurkin I.G., Tsvetkov V.Ya. Geomarketing and GIS // Information Technologies, No.7, 1998. p.11-13.
231. Tsvetkov V.Ya. Tasks of geomarketing // Izvestiya vysokikh uchebnykh obrazovaniya. Geodesy and aerial photography. - 2000. - №5. - c.146-154.
232. Oznamets V.V. Geomarketing and geoservice: Monograph. - Saarbruken.: Palmarium Academic Publishing, 2020. -177 c.
233. Zatyagalova V.V. Geoinformation approach in monitoring of sea pollution from remote sensing data from space // Earth Sciences. - 2-2012.-

c.80-85.
234. Rozenberg I.N., Tsvetkov V.Ya. The Geoinformation approach // Eurupean Journal of Natural History. - 2009. - №5. - p.102 -103
235. Tsvetkov V.Ya. Fundamentals of geoinformation modelling // Izvestiya vysokikh uchebnykh obrazovaniya. Geodesy and aerial photography. - 1999. - №4. - c.147 -157
236. Akhralov S. S. et al. Geoinformation technologies and methods of mathematical modelling in hydrogeological research //Geographic information systems and technologies. InterCartoInterGIS. - 2020. - T. 26. - C. 240-252.
237. Savinykh V.P. Geoinformation modelling in space research // Educational resources and technologies - 2017. -3 (20). - c.109-117.
238. Lototskii V.L. Spatial information modelling // Educational resources and technologies. - 2016. - 3 (15). - c.114-122.
239. Kupriyanov A. O. Digital modelling in underground geodetic works // Educational resources and technologies. - 2015. - №4 (12). - c.57-65.
240. Oznamets V .V. Geoinformation semasiological modelling // Educational resources and technologies. - 2022. - № 2 (39). - C.68-75.
241. Sarycheva L. Using GMDH in ecological and socio-economical monitoring problems //Systems Analysis Modelling Simulation. - 2003. - T. 43. - №. 10. - C. 1409-1414.
242. Barzegar M. et al. MEMS technology and applications in geotechnical monitoring: a review //Measurement Science and Technology. - 2022. - T. 33. - №. 5. - C. 052001.
243. Todorova A.I. Application of geoinformatics in geoecology // Slavic Forum. 2023, 1(39). C. 358-362.
244. Raev, V.K. Dynamic geoinformatics // Slavic Forum. 2022, 2(36). C. 195-205
245. Silin Y. P., Animitsa E. G. Evolution of the paradigm of regional economy //Journal of new economy. - 2020. - T. 21. - №. 1. - C. 5-28.
246. Bakhareva N.A. Synergetics of spatial information // Slavic Forum - 2014. - 1(5). - c.25 -32.
247. Gospodinov S.G. Geoinformational management of real estate. - Saarbruken, 2023. -141 c.
248. Shaitura S.V. Information situation in geoinformatics// Educational resources and technologies. - 2016. - №5 (17). - c.103-108.
249. Abatecola G. et al. Real estate management: past, present, and future research directions //International Journal of Globalisation and Small Business. - 2013. - T. 5. - №. 1-2. - C. 98-113.
250. Tsvetkov V. Ya. Corporate Governance // Modern Management

Technologies. ISSN 2226-9339. - №4 (100).
251. van der Voordt T. Facilities management and corporate real estate management: FM/CREM or FREM? //Journal of Facilities Management. - 2017.
252. Appel-Meulenbroek R., Omar A. J. Branding theory contributions to corporate real estate management //A Handbook of Management Theories and Models for Office Environments and Services. - Routledge, 2021. - C. 129-139.
253. V. Ya. Tsvetkov, Resource Method of Information System Life Cycle Estimation // European Journal of Technology and Design. - 2014. № 2 (4). p.8691.
254. Rogova A. V., Krivoruchko K. Yu. V., Krivoruchko K. Yu. Life cycle management of real estate objects on the basis of BIM-technologies //Investments, urban planning, real estate as drivers of socio-economic development of the territory and improving the quality of life of the population. - 2022. - C. 223-228.
255. Ponyavina N. A., Zubareva Y. V., Zuev E. A. Application of IOT at the stage of operation of real estate objects // Construction and Real Estate. - 2018. - T. 1. - №. 2-1. - C. 29-33
256. Ratcliffe J., Stubbs M., Keeping M. Urban planning and real estate development. - Routledge, 2021/.
257. Bogoutdinov B.B., Tsvetkov V.Ya. Application of the model of complementary resources in investment activity // Vestnik of Mordovian University. -2014. - T. 24. № 4. - c.103-116
258. Jiang F., Kim K. A. Corporate governance in China: A survey //Review of Finance. - 2020. - T. 24. - №. 4. - C. 733-772.
259. Bolshakov N. et al. As-built BIM in real estate management: the change of paradigm in digital transformation of economy //IOP Conference Series:
Materials Science and Engineering. - IOP Publishing, 2020. - T. 940. - №. 1. - C.012017
260. Tao F. Performance analysis of real estate management entities based on DEA model and BP neural network model //Journal of Physics: Conference Series. - IOP Publishing, 2021. - T. 1744. - №. 2. - C. 022025
261. Munawar H. S. et al. Big data and its applications in smart real estate and the disaster management life cycle: A systematic analysis //Big Data and Cognitive Computing. - 2020. - T. 4. - №. 2. - C. 4
262. Rothschild-Elyassi G., Koehler J., Simon J. Actuarial justice //The handbook of social control. - 2018. - C. 194-206

263. Mirdjalilova D. S., Ziyayev M. K. Ways to improve real estate management based on surveying services //Theoretical & Applied Science. - 2020. - №. 1. - C. 156-162.
264. Bolshakov N. et al. Digital Asset in the System of Real Estate Management //E3S Web of Conferences. - EDP Sciences, 2021. - T. 263. - C. 04039.
265. Guarini M. R., Battisti F., Chiovitti A. A methodology for the selection of multi-criteria decision analysis methods in real estate and land management processes //Sustainability. - 2018. - T. 10. - №. 2. - C. 507.
266. Bernhold T., Wiesweg N. The use of key Key Performance Indicators in Real Estate Management A stocktaking along the CREM maturity level //The proceedings of the 20th EuroFM Research Symposium 2021. - 2021.
267. Tsvetkov V.Ya. Development of management technologies // State Counsellor. - 2015. - №4(12). - c.5-10.
268. Tsipinova B. S., Astakhova I. A., Ashinov Y. N. State regulation of land and property relations // Science, education and innovation for agro-industrial complex: state, problems and prospects. - 2018. - C. 259263.
269. Andrusov A., Svetlov E. Commercial management of real estate on the basis of key performance indicators // Management Accounting and Finance. - 2005. - №. 4. - C. 38-46.
270. Greenberg A., Gorbachev N. Information technologies of management. - Litres, 2022.
271. Kornilkov S. V. et al. Specifying the approaches to geoinformation monitoring to assess the development dynamics of mining enterprises as natural- technological systems // Izvestia vysshee obrazovaniya vysshee obrazovaniya. Gornyj zhurnal. - 2020. - №. 8. - C. 41-51.
272. Savinykh V.P. State of Space Geoinformatics. Monographic article // Slavic Forum. 2021, 2(32). C.7-17.
273. Tsvetkov V.Ya. Methods and systems of video information processing and presentation. - Moscow: SCST, VNTICentre, 1991. - 113 c.
274. Shayekhov I. M., Bikmullina I. I. Organisation of visual data representation // Vestnik of Technological University. - 2019. - T. 22. - №. 6. - C. 167-169
275. Lvovich Ya. E. E., Preobrazhensky A. P. Characteristics of data storage in corporate systems // Bulletin of the Voronezh Institute of High Technologies. - 2020. - №. 1. - C. 31-33.
276. Stroganova I. A. Repository-a new institution of the OTC derivatives market. - 2019.
277. Savinykh V.P., Solovyov I.V., Tsvetkov V.Ya. Development of the

national infrastructure of spatial data on the basis of the development of cartographic and geodesic fund of the Russian Federation // Izvestiya vysokikh uchebnykh uchebnykh obrazovaniye. Geodesy and aerial photography. - 2011. - №5. - c.85-91.

278. Mahmoud Ibrahim M. Real Estate Management System. - October University for Modern Sciences and Arts, 2019

279. Tsvetkov V.Ya., Bulgakov C.B., Titov E.K., Rogov I.E. Metamodelling in geoinformatics // Information and Space. 2020. - №1. -c .112-119.

280. Zaitseva O. V. Spatial metamodelling // Slavic Forum. V. Spatial metamodelling // Slavic Forum. 2021, 3(33). C.57-68/

281. Gross M., Zrobek R. Good governance in some public real estate management systems //Land Use Policy. - 2015. - T. 49. - C. 352-364

282. Zavadskas E. K. et al. An integrated assessment of the municipal buildings' use including sustainability criteria //Sustainable Cities and Society. - 2021. - T. 67. - C. 102708.

283. Buck K. D., Summers J. K., Smith L. M. Investigating the relationship between environmental quality, socio-spatial segregation and the social dimension of sustainability in US urban areas //Sustainable Cities and Society. - 2021. - T. 67. - C. 102732.

284. Kudzh C.A., Gurtov B.S. State management of educational organisations' real estate: a monograph. - Moscow. MAKS Press, 2023. - 152 c.

285. Tsvetkov V.Ya., Tyagunov A.M. Information needs in the information realm // In Proceedings: AIP Conference Proceedings. 2. Cep. "Proceedings of the II International Conference on Advances in Materials, Systems and Technologies, CAMSTech-II 2021" 2022. C. 050004.

286. Tsvetkov V.Ya. Information-measuring systems and technologies in geoinformatics. - Moscow: MAKS Press, 2016. - 94 c.

287. Tsvetkov V.Y., Bolbakov R.G., Mordvinov V.A., Plotmikov S.B.. Discarding abnormal measurements // In: Informatics and Cybernetics in Intelligent Systems. Proceedings of 10th Computer Science On-line Conference 2021, Vol. 3. Proceedings of 10th Computer Science On-line Conference. Cep. "Lecture Notes in Networks and Systems 2021. C. 710-717

288. Hadas T. et al. Impact and implementation of higher-order ionospheric effects on precise GNSS applications //Journal of Geophysical Research: Solid Earth. - 2017. - T. 122. - №. 11. - C. 9420-9436.

289. Kupriyanov A.O., Tsvetkov V.Ya. Application of GNSS in applied geoinformatics // Educational Resources and Technologies. - 2016. - 1 (13). -

c.135-144.
290. Wang N. et al. Refinement of global ionospheric coefficients for GNSS applications: Methodology and results //Advances in Space Research. - 2019. - T. 63. - №. 1. - C. 343-358.
291. Ozherel'eva T.A. Models of data relations in the information field // International Journal of Applied and Fundamental Research. - 2015. - № 2 - C. 22-24.
292. Potapov A. S. Information situation and information position in the information field // Slavic Forum. - 2017. - 1(15). - c.283-289.
293. Tsvetkov V. Ya. Information Space, Information Field, Information Environment // European researcher. 2014. № 8-1(80). p.1416-1422
294. Spesivtsev A. A. Global navigation satellite systems // Approximation approaches and analysis of geophysical data. - 2020. - C. 26-26/
295. Veselov V. V. et al. On the necessity of using permanent reference base stations for cadastral works //Models and technologies of nature management (regional aspect).
- 2019. - №. 1 (8). - C. 142/
296. Quan Y. et al. Convolutional neural network based multipath detection method for static and kinematic GPS high precision positioning //Remote Sensing. - 2018. - T. 10. - №. 12. - C. 2052.
297. Jamieson M., Gillins D. T. Comparative analysis of online static GNSS postprocessing services // Journal of surveying engineering. - 2018. - T. 144. - №. 4. - C. 05018002.
298. Defaria C. et al. Cinematic mastering for virtual reality and augmented reality : patent pending. 16712820 US. - 2020.
299. GOST R 55536- 2013 Global navigation satellite systems. Methods and technologies of geodetic works. General requirements for fundamental geodetic parameters. Moscow, Standardinform, 2013.
300. Bugajewski L., M. Tsvetkov V.Ya. Geoinformation systems. - M.: "Zlatoust", 2000 - 224 p.
301. Tsvetkov V. Ya. Semantic environment of information units // European researcher. 2014, № 6-1 (76). p. 1059-1065.
302. Ozhereleva T. A. Systematics for information units // European Researcher. 2014, no. 11/1 (86), pp. 1894-1900.
303. Tsvetkov, V. Ya. Semantics of information units (in Russian) // Uspekhi sovremennoi naukhestvosnaniya. - 2007. - №10. - c.103-104.
304. Tsvetkov V.Ya. Information units as a means of building a picture of the world // International Journal of Applied and Fundamental Research. -

2014. - № 8 -4. - c. 36-40.
305. Kudzh S.A., Tsvetkov V.Y. Information educational units // Distance and virtual learning-2014. - №1(79). - c.2431
306. Barr M., Wells C. Category theory for computing science. - New York : Prentice Hall, 1990.
307. Rydeheard D. E., Burstall R. M. Computational category theory. - Englewood Cliffs : Prentice Hall, 1988. - T. 152.
308. Goldblatt P., Grishin V. H., Shokurov V. V. Topos: categorical analysis of logic. - Mir, 1983.
309. Eilenberg S., MacLane S. Cohomology theory in abstract groups. I //Annals of mathematics. - 1947. - C. 51-78.
310. Lachowski G. et al. On the complexity of the standard translation of lambda calculus into combinatory logic //Reports on Mathematical Logic. - 2018. - №. 53. - C. 19-42.
311. Ahmed M. U. et al. A multivariate multiscale fuzzy entropy algorithm with application to uterine EMG complexity analysis //Entropy. - 2017. - T. 19. - №. 1. - C. 2.
312. Tsvetkov, V.Ya.; Moshchil, V.Ya. Decision-making under risk conditions in geoinformation technologies // Izvestiya vysshee obrazovaniye vysshee obrazovaniye. Geodesy and aerial photography. 1999. № 4. C. 158-165.
313. Deshko I.P., Tsvetkov V. Ya. Physical complexity of algorithms. In Proceedings of the 10th th Computer Science On-line Conference "Software Engineering and Algorithms". Proceedings of 10 th Computer Science On-line Conference "Software Engineering and Algorithms". 2021. C. 369-374.
314. Tsvetkov V. Ya. Ya., Buravtsev A.V. Conceptual programming in GIS development // In Proceedings: IOP Conference Series: Earth and Environmental Science. Krasnoyarsk Science and Technology City Hall of the Russian Union of Scientific and Engineering. Krasnoyarsk, 2021. C. 32028.
315. Lee J. H., Ostwald M. J., Gu N. Measuring Cognitive Complexity //Design Thinking: Creativity, Collaboration and Culture. - Springer, Cham, 2020. - C. 85-110
316. Scott J. On the Topological Complexity of Maps //arXiv preprint arXiv:2011.10646. - 2020
317. E K Titov1 and V Ya Tsvetkov. Accumulated reliability of information hardware and software systems, 2020. IOP Conf. Series: Materials Science and Engineering, 919 (2020) 022055, doi:10.1088/1757-899X/919/6/022055.
318. Raev V.K. Mythological models as a research tool // Slavic Forum. -

2020. - 3(29). -c.56-66.
319. Schneider, M., & Somers, M. (2006). Organisations as complex adaptive systems: Implications of Complexity Theory for leadership research. The Leadership Quarterly, 17(4), 351-365.
320. Schilling R. et al. Revisiting the impact of information systems architecture complexity: a complex adaptive systems perspective. - 2017.
321. Nomokonov I.B., Tsvetkov V.Ya. Multidimensionality informativeness. // Distance and Virtual Learning. - 2015. - №12(102). - c.74-80
322. Kudzh S.A., Tsvetkov V.Ya., Nomokonov I.B.. Informativeness of visual models // In Proceedings: Journal of Physics: Conference Series. Krasnoyarsk, Russian Federation, 2020. C. 32009
323. Tsvetkov V.Ya. Spatial logic in geoinformatics // Vector GeoSciences. 2020. T. 3. № 2. C. 91-100.
324. Aiello M., Pratt-Hartmann I., Van Benthem J. What is Spatial Logic? // Handbook of spatial logics. - Springer, Dordrecht, 2007. - p. 1-11.
325. Tsvetkov V.Ya. Spatial knowledge and spatial logic // ITNOU: Information technologies in science, education and management. - 2019.- № 3 (13). - c. 17-26.
326. Tsvetkov V.Ya. Spatial knowledge and spatial logic // ITNOU: Information technologies in science, education and management. - 2019. - № 3 (13). - c.17-26.
327. Nomokonov I.B. Spatial logic in radial diagnostics // Slavic Forum. - 2020. - 3(29). -c.129-139.
328. Tsvetkov V.Y. The use of additional conditions in photogrammetric constructions // Lecture Notes in Civil Engineering. 2021. T. 151 LNCE. C. 8592.
329. Tsvetkov V.Ya., Selmanova N.N. Application of statistical method for calculating the areal object area // Perspectives of Science and Education. 2018. № 1 (31). C. 214-218.
330. Lonsky I.I., Bulgakov S.V., Tsvetkov V.Ya. Probabilistic logic in computer science // In Proceedings: AIP Conference Proceedings. Melville, New York, United States of America, 2021. C. 50060.
331. Kamynina N.R., Oznamets V.V., Tsvetkov V.Y.. Landing sites selection for the returned spacecraft // In Proceedings: AIP Conference Proceedings. 2. Cep. "Proceedings of the II International Conference on Advances in Materials,
Systems and Technologies, CAMSTech-II 2021" 2022. C. 060004.
332. Nomokonov I.B. Visual models and their semantics // Educational

resources and technologies. - 2021. - № 4 (37). - C. 53-60.
333. Nomokonov I.B., Tsvetkov V.Ya. Multidimensionality of informativeness. // Distance and virtual learning. - 2015. - №12(102). - c.74-80.
334. Tsvetkov V.Ya., Subocheva A.O., Ryazantseva M.V. Cognitive logic in management // In Proceedings: AIP Conference Proceedings. Melville, New York, United States of America, 2021. C. 50050.
335. Elsukov P. Yu. Cognitive logic // Slavic Forum. -2020. - 3(29). -c.87-95.
336. Moratz, R., & Ragni, M. Qualitative spatial reasoning about relative point position. // Journal of Visual Languages & Computing, 2008, 19(1), 75-98
337. Randell D. A., Cui Z., Cohn A. G. A spatial logic based on regions and connectivity //KR. - 1992. - V.92. - C. 165-176.
338. Del Bimbo A., Vicario E., Zingoni D. A spatial logic for symbolic description of image contents // Journal of Visual Languages & Computing. - 1994. - V.5. - №. 3. - C. 267-286
339. Tsvetkov V.Ya. Geoinformation systems and technologies - M.: Finance and Statistics, 1998. -288 c.
340. Bogoutdinov B.B., Tsvetkov V.Ya. Application of the model of complementary resources in investment activity // Vestnik of Mordovian University. -2014. - T. 24. № 4. - c.103-116
341. Eckert M., Joerg W. On the nature of maps and map logic //Bulletin of the American Geographical Society. - 1908. - V.40. - №. 6. - C. 344-351.
342. Kravets E. A. Cartographic logic (analysis of the issues of the state and environmental protection): monograph - M.: Izd-vo MIIGAiK, 2010.160s.
343. Lyutiy A.A. Map language: essence, system, functions. - 2nd ed. -
M.: GEOS, 2002. - 327 c.
344. Bertrand Russell. Vagueness. In John Slater, editor (1923) , *Essays on Language, Mind, and Matter 1919-26,* The Collected Papers of Bertrand Russell, pages 145 - 154. Unwin Hyman, London
345. Tsvetkov V. Ya. Spatial Information Models // European researcher. №10-1(60). c.2386-2392
346. Tarski, Alfred (1956). Foundations of the geometry of solids. In *Logic, Semantics, and Metamathematics*, pages 24-29. Clarendon Press, Oxford.
347. Savinykh V.P. Conceptual blending in geocognition // Slavic Forum. - 2017. - 2(16). - c.19-24.
348. Rosenberg, I. N.; Tsvetkov, V. Ya. Conceptual spatial blending in the

analysis of transport infrastructure objects // Railways Science and Technology. - 2019. T.3.- 3(11). - c.3-16

MIX
Papier aus verantwortungsvollen Quellen
Paper from responsible sources
FSC® C105338

Printed by Books on Demand GmbH, Norderstedt / Germany